Step by Step with Joy

by
Karen Eleuteri

authorHOUSE™

1663 LIBERTY DRIVE, SUITE 200
BLOOMINGTON, INDIANA 47403
(800) 839-8640
WWW.AUTHORHOUSE.COM

First published by AuthorHouse 03/08/05

ISBN: 1-4184-8211-0 (e)
ISBN: 1-4184-8210-2 (sc)
ISBN: 1-4184-8209-9 (dj)

Printed in the United States of America
Bloomington, Indiana

This book is printed on acid-free paper.

Dedication

To Joy's children:
Jacob, Elizabeth, and Peter

and also to Joy's devoted sister,
my beloved daughter and friend:
Tina

Acknowledgements

First, thank you, God, for showing us your love, day after day, in your marvelous, mysterious and miraculous ways.

And then many thanks to a remarkable group of people who helped me take my memories, stories and emotions and turn them into this book. They all encouraged me to write Joy's story, pushed me when I didn't think I could write another word, and throughout gave their time and talents to turn a manuscript into a book.

They are: Lynnan Ware whose sharp eye was most helpful early on; Isabelle Gundaker, a retired Rowan University writing coordinator and instructor, who was my kind, tough and very organized editor; Linda Artlip who proofed the manuscript, made it look like a book and then designed the cover I had dreamed of. Everyone needs friends like these!

And finally, and most particularly, thank you, Larry, my beloved husband: for your love and support, your encouragement, your belief in me and your appreciation of my call to serve the Lord who most certainly blessed me by giving me such a wonderful husband and dear friend. I love you.

Table of Contents

Chapter One

Here Comes the Bride

The organ began to play. The guests stood and eagerly turned to face the back of the church as the bride came into view. She looked beautiful. Her exquisite floor-length strapless gown fell to the floor as its silk panels elegantly shaped her slender figure. Her transparent veil enveloped her as it flowed from her perfectly coiffed hair down to her bare shoulders then gracefully descended to lie in gentle folds at the hem of her gown. Concealed under her wedding gown were the prostheses that enabled her to stand and walk and the designer sneakers that she chose to wear for fit and balance.

The presenter of the bride was her four-year-old son looking debonair and ever so grown up in a miniature black tuxedo that matched the groom's. His dark brown hair was neatly styled to manage his beautiful but unruly curls. His feet, in rented shiny black shoes, shuffled eagerly displaying the excitement this young boy was feeling. After all, today was a very important day for him too. He was getting a new Daddy who loved him and was committed to caring and providing for him. Now, as the music signaled them, the radiant bride and her enthusiastic presenter began the walk down the aisle hand in hand.

The groom, even more handsome than usual in his black tuxedo, was awaiting them. Tall with dark freshly trimmed hair, his face beamed with love for his bride and new son. This special man was specifically chosen for them; there was no doubt. Only God could have placed this man in their lives the way He did to bring about this happy beginning.

Now, every eye was on the bride as she miraculously glided down the aisle in graceful motion. Friends and family in attendance marveled that she was actually walking…and down the aisle at that! Tears streamed down many faces as they remembered her as the six-year-old girl who contracted a rare and life-threatening case of chicken pox, lost both her legs and was never expected to walk again.

Even more poignant to one guest was the memory of this little girl who wondered after seeing her amputated legs, "But who will marry me?"

And, now, we all knew the answer to that question.

§§§

As the mother of the bride, with the planning and preparation finally behind me, I could now relax and reflect on the events that led to this exciting day. Even at this moment while I stood, anticipating my daughter's every movement to Richard Wagner's famous *Wedding March*, my thoughts went back to a time when this day seemed to be only a dream a mother has for her daughter.

Chapter Two

Joy's Primary Foothold

My mind wandered all the way back to my own childhood and to the people who undoubtedly influenced how Joy was raised. I was born Karen Elizabeth Fowler on March 31, 1948, in "up-state" Pottsville, Pennsylvania to Elizabeth Mary (nee Wolfgang) and Edward Francis Fowler. I was their second child. Their first born, Edward Jr., was 2½ years older than I. Thirteen years after my birth and much to my mother's surprise and much to my delight, they had another daughter, Kay. This tiny infant filled our home with all the happiness that accompanies a new baby.

My mother, typical of her generation, was a devoted wife and quite the traditional motherly type. Although it was my father who was the head of the family, my mother was the wisdom and strength behind the man. She was a registered nurse, an accomplishment of which she was very proud and a career she cherished. Nevertheless, she gave up her career after my sister was born to stay home with her and to help run the family business. Although my mother was committed to doing whatever her family needed, giving up her dreams and her career in nursing was a tremendous sacrifice she willingly made for her family.

I was outgoing like my father, but it was my mother who really influenced me. My mother's church and its teachings of the "Good Book" played a large part in my mother's upbringing. My grandmother, Edith Krah Wolfgang, played the piano at their local church and the family attended regularly and became very accustomed to being in the presence of God.

It was my mother's faith, her firm foundation and purpose of life to which I gravitated. Her own life taught her the discipline one needs to survive. When she was a very young woman, she lost her father. He was a foreman or fire-boss for Reading Coal and Iron Company. As was common in those days, local people would dig their own mining holes adjacent to and connecting to the mining shafts of the coal company. These were called bootleggers' holes. The bootleggers were illegally removing coal from the strain that belonged to the company. However, these were hard times in 1940 and some of these local people were not removing coal to profit from it, but to keep their own families warm. This is not to excuse the deed, but to describe the times.

On this given Sunday around dinnertime, my grandfather, Andrew Wolfgang, received a phone call telling him that there was an accident in one of the bootleg holes. He set out to help. An accident in the mines usually meant that the mine caved in and men were trapped below. My grandfather insisted that he be the one to be lowered into the mine to find and rescue the trapped men. A rope was tied around him, a safety line, to keep track of him as well as help raise him out of the mine along with those who were trapped.

He was slowly lowered into the dark hole when, all at once, his rope went taut, indicating a lifeless form at the other end. Those above ground assumed my grandfather had found the men trapped in the mine and had tied one of the men to his rope. The tautness of the rope indicated that in all likelihood, the trapped miner was dead. As the men above ground pulled on the rope to bring the person out of the caved-in mineshaft, they were horrified to see my grandfather's lifeless body at the end of the rope. Either carbon monoxide gas from the mine or a heart attack had killed him. He was 40 years old and left a wife and four children: 19-year-old Elizabeth ("Betty", my mother), 17-year-old Donald, 15-year-old Marshall and 13-year-old Doris.

As a young girl, my mother was all too familiar with death. She came from Lavelle, a very small town in Pennsylvania. Many of the residents of this "valley" were her relatives. They too worked in the coal mines. Several young men lost their lives due to the dangerous working conditions in the mines. In this small town, everyone knew everyone else and they depended on and trusted each other implicitly. The values and principles these people lived were the principles set down in the Bible. They knew right from wrong and lived and raised their families on these principles. When someone passed away, the whole town mourned the loss.

Mother was all too aware of the mourning process and the wake or viewing of the body before the burial, along with the responsibility of caring for the family both financially and personally afterwards. Her town and its widows were faced with these problems throughout her childhood. The "wake" was often held in the home of the deceased. After the undertaker embalmed the body, it would be delivered back to the home for the viewing. There were practical reasons for holding these visitations at home: the cost of holding the viewing at the funeral home in town was too expensive, and transportation was not available to everyone to get there. Out of respect, the tradition was that the deceased was never left alone, even throughout the night.

Corpses always made my mother uncomfortable. Yet, as a dutiful daughter, she took her turn staying up alone with the body. As she prayed all night beside her father's corpse, the weight of the world seemed to be on her shoulders. She pondered how the family would eat and keep up with the expenses of running a household and raising young children now that her father was gone and there was no one to provide the necessary income for the family. My mother offered to quit nursing school and go to work to help support the family, but my grandmother reminded her daughter that the Lord would provide for the family in this time of tragedy. Mom was informed that she was to finish nursing school.

My grandmother and her children had to depend on God for everything since there was no big life insurance policy to cash in, no workman's compensation, no lawsuit, and no settlement; just a meager amount of money monthly on which to live. Nevertheless, the family survived financially and the very day after graduating, my mother took a 7-day-a-week private-duty nursing job. In my mother's view, being a nurse was a way for her to support her mother and siblings along with sharing her Christian faith through her own compassion and charity. Being a nurse meant everything to her. My mother's Christian values and strong work ethic governed the standard of living in our home. As her daughter, I learned these lessons well.

Following the traditional career trend of both my church and home, after graduating from Moorestown (NJ) Senior High School in 1966, I attended Philadelphia College of Bible, now called Philadelphia Bible University, in Philadelphia, Pennsylvania. After completing two years at the college and then a three-year nursing program at Pennsylvania School of Nursing in Philadelphia, I would have completed the requirements to become a missionary nurse.

However, I quit nursing school shortly after arriving as I just didn't feel I was on the right career path. My real desire was to be a physician, but in my background a girl could only become a teacher or a nurse so I could not begin to imagine how I could become a physician. Being impatient to begin my life's journey, I chose to become a self-employed businesswoman.

The type of business I would own did not actually matter to me, but I was aware that the beauty industry was welcoming to women as business owners, commonly called salon owners. So in the fall of 1968, I walked from 8th and Spruce Street where I was in nursing school to a beauty school at 13th and Market Street. After discovering that the course to become a cosmetologist (hairstylist) took only 9 months, I enrolled.

At the time I was dating Ken Spering who was eight years older than I. In the summer between my freshman and sophomore years of college, I had worked at an army ammunitions plant where we met. He was a maintenance supervisor, and I was impressed with his strong work ethic and his extensive knowledge of building structures and maintaining equipment. Ken also had a fancy red sports car and money to spend on nice restaurants and entertainment, which I thoroughly enjoyed.

Ken was the third child in a family of six children. His father, Herbert Spering, was a career sergeant in the Army, and his mother Dorothy, known to all as Dottie, stayed at home and cared for their large family. Herb and Dottie decided to make Pemberton, New Jersey, their permanent home after Herb, who was stationed at Fort Dix, New Jersey, retired from the Army.

By the time I met Ken, his family was quite large since all of his siblings were married with children. When the whole family got together, it was such great fun. With the added bonus of Dottie's terrific Italian cooking, there was always plenty of great food and drink to help celebrate their family's many special occasions. Although Ken often drank too much at these celebrations and enjoyed having a few beers after work a few nights a week, I accepted this behavior as part of his need to unwind.

I was irresistibly drawn to Ken's attitude of casualness, excitement and spontaneity which seemed a welcomed change from the fundamental religious seriousness and restrictive lifestyle I had known. Ken and I decided to marry in 1970.

Chapter Three

Joyful Dreams

In 1972 when I was 24 years old, Ken and I bought a piece of property in Eastampton, New Jersey, and built a house with a hairstyling salon on the lower level so I could open my own salon. Our only child, our daughter Tina, was two years old. I hired a wonderful woman who cared for her upstairs in our home while I worked downstairs. Tina often visited with the clients and they would often arrive for their appointments with some little treat or gift that made Tina feel very special. Working in the same building as my home was a great way for me to work. I was "home" with my daughter yet had my own business and interesting clients and stimulating conversation filling my life. Although it was a very small business, I really enjoyed being my own boss.

On June 2, 1975, Joy was born. Like her sister, Tina, Joy was born prematurely because my placenta was small and she was not getting enough nourishment. However, I was only in labor a few hours before she was born. She was a healthy, fully developed, beautiful little girl. Her father and I agreed on the name Joy, which came from the words of a song I used to sing in Sunday School, "Jesus and Others and You, What a wonderful way to spell J O Y". Her middle name, Ellen, was chosen because it is my sister Kay's middle name. Joy was an easy baby who was pleasant and whose routine care was not unusually demanding.

Within the first year after her birth, I began looking into opening a chain of hairstyling salons. With this in mind, I planned to move the salon out of our home and into a shopping center a few miles away in Mount Holly, facing a busy highway. My husband and I had big dreams and plans, but no money to hire a contractor. Therefore, once Ken and I signed the lease on the building where the new salon was to be located, we immediately began working to make the space suitable for a hair salon. Ken and I would put in our regular full workday and then go to the new salon location at night to put up walls, paint, and get the plumbing and

Joy at 2 years-of-age

electrical ready for the salon to open. My parents would also come every evening to work into the wee hours of the morning to help do whatever they could. After a few months of hard work, we moved the salon out of our house and into the shopping center.

Then in 1978, Ken and I bought the dry cleaning business next door to the salon so that we could both be self-employed. Owning our own businesses was designed to give us the flexibility we wanted for our family.

The new salon and the dry cleaning business were located around the corner from Burlington County Memorial Hospital (now called Virtua) in Mount Holly, New Jersey. In 1978, the hospital hired a new young CEO, David Hunter. David and most of his administration became clients of mine at the salon. It wasn't long until many of the doctors, nurses and hospital personnel also became salon customers, which gave me an enjoyable connection to the medical profession. Dr. William (Terry) Kane, a good friend of Dave's, was soon recruited to join the team. Terry was the new Director of Medical Affairs and in charge of the Family Practice Residency Program. Terry became our family doctor. Ken and I became good friends with Dave and his wife, Mary, and Terry and his wife, Noreen. I quickly became involved in the hospital auxiliary and various committees, raising money and supporting the hospital. I was thrilled to be a part of it. The new friends I was making through my association with the hospital would become invaluable to my husband and me in our own medical nightmare just a few years later.

In 1980, we opened our second salon in Moorestown. Ken and I were good business partners. He did all the construction of the salons and the general maintenance of the businesses while I managed the staff, did the planning, and managed the finances.

While putting together the handbook of policies for the staff of the new salon, I became even more mindful of the changes that were occurring in the workplace for women. A woman's income was now necessary to support her family and no longer a meager addition to the family's income.

I was also reminded of my own role which was expanding more and more into both provider for and caregiver of our daughters as Ken began to stop regularly after work for a drink leaving the girls and me to fend for ourselves. These unexpected changes for me required additional energy to meet new demands, yet I was still highly motivated to make our dreams a reality. Ken was still project oriented and was able to accomplish projects relating to the businesses, but he began neglecting the day-to-day responsibilities of our family for his other interests.

However, for me, along with the role reversal going on in my home, there were other fundamental changes I was contemplating. I began questioning my relationship with the church. At a time in my life when I really needed the church's support and compassion, the church directive was, "Women, obey your husbands." I could not conform to this mandate since things had changed so drastically in my own home. I began to doubt the purpose of the church in my life and made the decision to stop going to church. I was not giving up on God, but on organized religion that attempted to speak for God in a manner in which I could not agree or apply to my life.

Nevertheless, the lessons and experiences of my own life made me very sensitive to the needs of our employees who were all women and whose income was vital to the well-being of their families. Since I could identify with them, I was careful to set company policies not just for the company's benefit, but also with full consideration of the needs of these women.

Our staff was made up of single, married, separated, co-habiting, divorced and remarried women. In this mix there were many children. I knew that the success of our businesses would mean food, clothing, homes, education, cars and hopefully much more for our staff members' families. I also realized that when a woman went to work, in her heart, mind and thoughts, she took her whole family with her.

Therefore, the company policy of Creative Image Salon was: if a staff member, her child or family member was sick and the stylist needed to go home or be absent, I always honored and seldom questioned that request. I understood that these women were also raising families, having babies, getting married, cooking for the holidays, and caring for sick people along with earning a living. The clients, being the special people that they were, supported the policies and understood the staff's needs as a whole. Each staff member was aware of what she had to do to get the job done. Each was expected to give her full attention and talents to the business and the clients when at work. I hired only people with good attitudes, knowing I could teach them the skills they needed to succeed if necessary. All stylists and support staff knew that they were not going to be fired just because they were pregnant, had children, got sick, or their families needed them.

To better allow stylists to take off when needed, I developed the practice of sharing clients between stylists, unlike the practices of most other salons. This meant if a stylist was not at work, I encouraged the client to go to another stylist who was equally talented. The client received an excellent service and then returned to the original stylist when that stylist returned to work. This concept kept the money on the books and kept the cash flow going even in the absence of a particular stylist. This practice also gave the stylists job security as no one was permitted to "steal the client."

Our work environment was purposely created to be friendly and family oriented and, although Ken and I continued to have someone care for the girls at our home while we worked, it was not uncommon for Tina and Joy to also spend time with us at the businesses. Our hours of work were long, and the businesses became their home away from home. Also, the salon staff and the clients became our extended family.

Tina acclimated to the businesses easily. It was not unusual to see her helping out in the drycleaners. By the age of seven, she would pull up a stool to stand on so that she could reach the counter to help a customer. Tina's nature is to be giving and selfless. Therefore she seemed to understand what we were trying to achieve as a family and, even as a very young child, joined in to help.

The same year we opened the new salon, my beloved father passed away. He had suffered from the effects of diabetes for a number of years and now a fatal heart attack took him home to be with the Lord. Shortly after my father's passing, my mother decided to move from the large homestead in Moorestown, and Ken and I purchased it from her. We moved the 10 miles from Eastampton to Moorestown just in time for Joy to start kindergarten. In our overall plan to succeed, we were ambitious and seemed to be right on track.

Tina & Joy

September 1978

Chapter Four

A Deadly Case of Chicken Pox

Being a working mother was especially difficult, at certain times. Whether to go to work or stay home with a sick child is always a difficult choice, and this was my dilemma on May 1, 1982. For a few days, Joy, now six years old, had been slightly feverish and out of sorts, so our family doctor, Terry Kane, stopped by the house that afternoon to check on Joy. Terry examined her to find that, along with her fever, malaise and loss of appetite, there were a few flat red spots on her stomach. Chicken pox, a common childhood disease, was the diagnosis. He instructed us what to expect from this disease. As he explained, more and more red spots would continue to develop over the next 3 to 4 days. These red spots would itch severely, but would crust over and scab in 6-8 hours. The scabs would last from 5-20 days. He also cautioned us that she was highly contagious. Nothing seemed unusual about this particular case of chicken pox. He explained how to care for her and we followed those instructions.

Joy seemed to be doing fine, but as a precaution, I asked my mother if the girls could come to her house that day instead of having the sitter at our home. It was Saturday, the busiest day of the week at the salon, and I just felt better with my mother's watchful nurse's eye on Joy. So, on his way to the dry cleaners, Ken dropped Tina and Joy off at Mom's house, which was just minutes around the corner from his business.

Mom invited us for dinner after work since we had to pick up the girls anyway. What a treat that was for me to have a delicious home-cooked meal with my family after working all week! Mom had relocated to a townhouse in Lumberton, New Jersey, which bordered Mount Holly where two of our businesses were located.

Mom had been ready to begin her life living alone after the death of our father. Everyone assumed that Mom would be unlikely to remarry because she was a rather shy individual. However, God had a different plan for her. William L. Love, Bill, a wonderful man Mom had known since grade school, respectfully expressed his sympathy and sent his regards on hearing of her husband's death. Unbeknownst to anyone, a match was being made in heaven and the two were married a year later.

Bill, whom we affectionately called Pop, had the same wonderful "upstate" Pennsylvania Dutch values and principles that our mother and father practiced. Having been raised by the same Christian standards and having attended the same Christ Evangelical Church as our ancestors, we could easily trust him with our mother's love and fondly welcomed him into our family. Bill was a retired railroad engineer who worked for the Reading Railroad for over 40 years and who had lost his first wife to cancer. Bill had one child, Bill Jr., who had two children, Courtney and Chip (William) and along with his wife, Dian and her two children, David and Michelle, our family happily increased.

Shortly after an enjoyable dinner with Mom and Pop, Ken and I and the girls went home. Joy still seemed to be feeling the same as she had earlier in the day. Nothing seemed to have changed. Joy was not a child who was ill often and seldom complained, so I was somewhat concerned at 10:30 that night when Joy told us her leg hurt. I looked at it and found marks like very faint webbing on her right thigh. Although it was late, I called my mother to see if she had noticed anything strange that day on Joy's leg. Had Joy fallen and hurt herself? Had she complained at all about her leg hurting? My mother said that nothing unusual had happened and that she did not see anything on Joy's leg. Being concerned grandparents, however, Mom and Pop immediately drove to our home to take a look at Joy's leg. No one could figure out what had happened. Ken and I could hear the concern in my mother's voice as she cautioned us while walking out the door for home, "Keep an eye on Joy."

We all went to bed. At 4 AM, Joy limped into our bedroom, again complaining about her leg hurting. We put her in bed with us, never dreaming that this was the last time she would walk on her own legs for the rest of her life. I again examined her leg and saw that the black and blue areas had gotten bigger. Still, her discomfort and the marks did not seem overly alarming. We discussed going to the hospital but decided to wait until the morning. At 7 AM, the marks had spread and appeared black and were now on both legs. Now they were the size of my hand fully extended and very black! Something was happening at a very rapid speed! Joy could no longer walk because of the pain. Now very alarmed and concerned, we gathered up both our daughters and sped the seven miles to the Burlington County Memorial Hospital, the hospital where many of the doctors, nurses and administrators came to my salon. I hoped and prayed that my friends at this hospital would help and that someone there would tell us, "It's going to be all right. Don't worry."

To my disappointment, on this Sunday morning, no one I knew personally was at the hospital. However, Dr. Joseph Maloney, the doctor who saw Joy this day, was in the same pediatric group as her regular pediatrician. He immediately attended to Joy. He drew blood for tests and did everything precisely as he should with a sense of urgency. His concern showed in his actions and on his face. Yet Ken and I had no idea what was going on. I called my parents to tell them that we were at the hospital and they arrived within minutes. After examining Joy and reading the reports, Dr. Maloney urged us to take her immediately to Children's Hospital of Philadelphia (CHOP). He had already called and the doctors there were awaiting her arrival. He implored us to leave immediately and drive her there ourselves. "Do not wait for an ambulance!" he pleaded. Ken gently lifted Joy into his arms as we all rushed to the car. We sped the 40 miles to CHOP.

By this time, Joy could not bend her legs because they had become so swollen. As Ken drove the car, I reclined my seat and held Joy on my lap, trying to keep her legs straight and still even over the bumps in the road. The least movement of her legs made her scream with pain. The black on her legs continued to spread and her feet were becoming discolored as well. Ken, Tina and I tried to keep our composure as we frantically wondered what was happening.

We arrived at the emergency entrance to CHOP. Two people in medical attire with somber expressions carefully and quickly took Joy from my arms, placed her on the stretcher and then whisked her away. As they were rushing her into the hospital, someone yelled back to inform us that Joy would be in the Intensive Care Unit on the 4th floor and we were to go there. Ken, Tina and I hurried there while Mom and Pop parked the car. When Ken, Tina and I arrived at Joy's room, we realized that Joy was placed in a room alone, in reverse isolation, so that she could not give the chicken pox or this other mysterious disease to the other children in the hospital.

Medical personnel were scurrying in and out of her room. It was now about 9 AM, and my brother and his wife, Ed and Carol Fowler, and their thirteen-year-old son, Tim, my sister and her husband,

Kay and Frank Bowker, arrived at the hospital and joined Ken, Tina, Mom, Pop and me on the 4th floor. Being a family of faith, we were already praying for Joy.

There was much confusion, but one thing was certain: no one is in an Intensive Care Unit of a hospital unless his or her condition is very serious. How were we to know that from this day, May 2, 1982, until sometime in late September, my husband and I would live in this hospital, day and night, with Joy. However, right now, all we could do was wait and pray.

Joy —— 1980

Chapter Five

12 Hours to Live

It seemed an eternity before one of the doctors came out of the room to tell us what was going on. He was a pediatric hematologist, Dr. Mortimer Poncz, a specialist in problems with blood diseases and disorders. He told us the shocking news that Joy had an unusual side effect of varicella (chicken pox), called purpura fulminans. He explained that it is an extremely rare blood disorder associated with this virus and that it causes antibodies to act in bizarre ways. The odds of contracting purpura fulminans were five million to one. The results of this complication are an overwhelming disorder of the circulatory system that paradoxically causes clotting and bleeding at the same time. Information was so scant regarding this condition that when the doctors at CHOP contacted other hospitals and doctors around the nation to inquire about this disorder, only one doctor responded. His comment was that he had seen purpura fulminans once before. He advised the doctors that in the one case that he had seen, the patient died within hours. Mortality overall in these cases exceeded 90%. Dr. Poncz then informed us that Joy had only 12 hours to live.

Instantly I was terrified and just as instantly I fought my terror with my instinct to survive. I began to look inside myself for the strength I would need. I recalled an experience I had as a little girl on the boardwalk in a storm back in 1954. I recalled how God calmed the storm within me then. I felt sure He could calm this storm as well.

When I was six years old, my family went to the shore, Seaside Heights, New Jersey, for one of the two vacations that we took during my childhood. Aunt Doris, Uncle Trucent and my cousin, Pat, went as well. One night after spending the day on the beach and jumping the waves in the ocean, we all went to the boardwalk, a place of rides for children, fun, food, bright lights, wheels of chance and plenty of excitement.

A very big storm came up out of nowhere. Sheets of rain were pouring down out of the sky. Everyone had to seek shelter. We chose the overhang above the stores along the boardwalk. From this vantage point we could still see and sometimes feel the raging storm. Lightning was flashing all around us. It was even scarier in the total darkness as the entire area was now blacked out. The rain continued to come down and blow with a fierceness I had never seen before. I was petrified!

My father and uncle had already walked ahead of us up the boardwalk to play some of the game wheels in hopes of winning a prize for each of the children, as my Uncle Trucent was very good at winning. Now that the storm had so suddenly erupted, we were separated from them. I was extremely concerned for my father and uncle since they were not with us. Suddenly, a verse of scripture came to my mind. It was a verse I had memorized in Sunday school. I knew God was speaking to me when He said:

> *"Trust in the Lord with all your heart,*
> *And lean not on your own understanding;*
> *In all your ways acknowledge Him;*
> *And He shall direct your paths."*
>
> Proverbs 3:5 & 6

These were not just words of comfort, but words of truth as well. I closed my eyes tightly and prayed, knowing God would realize how terrified I was and how seriously I needed His help. Then silently, and with the sincere faith and trust of a six-year-old child, I prayed…

"Please, Jesus, help! This storm really scares me!
Please, please don't let anything happen to my Daddy
and Uncle Trucent.
You said that I can trust You to help me
and I need Your help right now! I am really scared! Amen.

God heard my prayer and answered it! Everything turned out perfectly that evening. The storm passed and my father and uncle returned safely with a parakeet in a cage. My Uncle Trucent once again had the winning touch. I do not remember what happened to the parakeet, since obviously my uncle could not divide it among three children. However, I clearly remember who my God was to me that evening. I trusted He was the same God who would be there for me now as I faced the biggest and most challenging storm in my life. And I knew He could win over this storm too! As Joy lay near death in the ICU Unit of Children's Hospital of Philadelphia, I realized that she was the same age I was when I first met God face to face on that boardwalk in Seaside Heights, New Jersey.

After my brief reflection, I next searched my memory hoping to find some hope from what I had read in the Bible. The Bible is not a self-help book, but a "God Will Help" book. In it God said I could trust Him with the details of my life, and if ever I needed His help with confusing and unclear details, it was now. Everything that I had learned to depend on — my problem solving ability, my ability to plan and execute, my emotional stability, and my physical strength — were all insignificant now. None of these human attributes were enough to save Joy's life. Having never had any experience before with a serious life-threatening illness, I absolutely needed strength and wisdom far greater than mine. I needed God.

Although I had already memorized many passages of scripture from the Bible on how to live successfully and confidently, I now had a much greater appreciation for these truths. God's book took on a whole new meaning for me. It was no longer just a book filled with amazing stories for children, it was a book filled with demonstrations and examples of the power and might of my God! Even with my heart so heavy and broken, I felt assured that He understood Joy's situation and would provide the answers to the questions that I didn't have the words to ask.

Philippians 4: 13, says,
"I can do all things through Christ who strengthens me."

Christ would give me the strength. And I needed to depend on that promise not just to help me get through this, but also to help me be victorious over it. I felt like war had just been declared and I needed to be readied for the battle. God's love was so powerful and sincere and filled with promises of comfort, help, courage and hope that I had to depend on Him for His help. There was no one else who could save Joy's life. With not even enough time to bow my head or close my eyes, as my heart silently wept, I prayed...

"Oh Father, please help us! I know You are here. And I know You know what is happening to us. But I do not. I have never felt this empty before, this uncertain, and this unclear, this

confused and frightened! I am totally lost and blinded by this. I cannot see my way even to the next moment. There are some things I do know and some things that I am certain of even now. I know You love me. I know You love Joy. I know You can hear my heart crying out to You even though it is broken.
I know You will answer.
Give me the strength to accept Your answer and the courage to do the right thing for her. I know You know what will happen next and what will happen tomorrow.
Give me peace in these truths.
Give me courage beyond my ability.
Give me hope beyond the words the doctors are speaking to us right now about Joy's expected death.
Help us do whatever it takes for her to survive these twelve hours. And Father, please empower these doctors with Your wisdom and let them know that You are here to help. Please don't let her die, Lord…please, she's just a little girl. My little girl."
In Jesus' name, Amen.

God heard my prayer. I was sure of that. I immediately felt more calm and strengthened to fight this battle. I was also sure that He knew the outcome of this event. Even more important, He had the power to change the event if it was His will. His love for and knowledge of Joy as a person began before mine. God says:

"Before I formed you in the womb I knew you."

Jeremiah 1:5

Therefore God knew this exact day would come when the life of this little 6-year-old child would be in His hands.

Chapter Six

Calling On God to Help

The clock was ticking on what were possibly Joy's last moments of life. I could become frozen in fear and let that emotion control me and keep God from helping or, since her life or death was only hours away, move quickly out of my own emotions and fears into the arms of Jesus who was waiting to help me.

Faith is about the unseen possibilities of the outcome of events. My intellect had to defer to my faith. There was nowhere else to turn. All indications were that this disease was so rare and deadly that few in the medical profession had seen it before. Where does a person turn then for answers and hope? I only knew of one thing to do. Deal with the impossible with the God who has already done the impossible in other events in history. He was real to me. I knew Him and I knew where to find Him. I knew of His amazing and supernatural powers.

God cares for and loves His people. The stories I had read in the Bible about Him were real historical events proving His ability to change the outcome of events that man could not change. I now needed Him to do the impossible for me. These may sound like strange thoughts at such moments in my life, but there was absolutely no one else to turn to. This was a hopeless situation that was going to result in Joy's death. Without supernatural intervention it was impossible to change its outcome. And I knew it.

I loved my children, but until this moment I had no idea how much.

The thought of Joy not going home ever again was unbearable. I instantly knew I would do anything it would take so that my feisty, bright, cute, blonde-haired daughter would return home with us. I just couldn't let go of the dreams I had for her. I still wanted to see the twinkle in her eyes from learning something new, her first date, her high school years, the prom, graduation, college, her first love, her wedding and her first child. My dreams and hopes had a whole lifetime planned for Joy as well as Tina. I had given my children life and I was willing to fight for it!

Yet I knew the threat of untimely death was all too real. My mind raced back to my own brush with death in 1967. One rainy Sunday morning in early December, my boyfriend Steve and I left for church from my home in my brother's red Chevy convertible. Only a block from my home, an uninsured motorist ran a stop sign, hitting the passenger side of our car at full speed where I was sitting, throwing both Steve and me from the car into a field. I landed away from the car about 65 feet, but Steve, even though he was driving, landed in the field just outside the car on the passenger's side. The other car then hit our car a second time and ran over Steve, killing him on impact; I was left with only a few superficial bruises.

Through my shock and heartbreak, I pondered the reasons I was saved and Steve was killed so tragically. Why did this happen? Why was I taken out of harm's way? Coincidence? Luck? Was it possible that God had placed me in Steve's life only to be a part of this terrible accident, his death and nothing more?

It became apparent to me that in God's plan people can die in what seems to be an improper order, the young dying sometimes before the elderly. God's feelings about life and death differ from ours.

God says,

"Precious in the sight of the Lord
Is the death of His saints."

Psalm 116:15

I realized that it is man who is afraid of death. To God, the return of a soul to Him is a precious homecoming. But I still hoped and prayed that Joy's homecoming would not be this night.

All of these thoughts went through my mind in what seems like an instant. I immediately set in motion a plan to do whatever I needed to do to keep Joy alive. God held the power and the answers. I needed to do all in my power to be a part of the solutions that He would implement. This was life and death and, as it turned out, everything in between. There was no Plan B; there was only God.

This turn of events in my life was as though I was casually moving along in a boat in a gentle river. The sun was shining on my face and I was enjoying the ride. But then unexpectedly there was a dangerous and deadly waterfall just ahead. And I was now in it, falling down into the body of water below, desperately trying to stay in the boat, and trying not to drown from the water that was engulfing me. All actions and reactions had to occur immediately and instinctively. I had to rely on the little experience I had and draw from it, however hidden it seemed to be in my mind. After the initial, "Oh, God, please help!" I had to start doing something instead of just hoping things would turn out all right. I had better find the oar and start paddling at some point and quickly get past the "Why me?" Only when I reached safety could I indulge myself and have an emotional reaction. Right now I just had to avoid panic, pray, and paddle.

As I sat on the bench outside of ICU, surrounded by my family and anticipating but dreading my child's death, I knew I had to find my oar, God, pray and start paddling. I knew the choice was either to become paralyzed with fear or to meet the challenge with God. I needed to know that whatever the outcome, I did the best I could. Then afterwards, I could have peace of mind knowing I did the right thing.

Chapter Seven

12 Hours Later: Hope

My family and I were gathered on the wooden benches outside the ICU making plans to remain at the hospital throughout these 12 hours, perhaps the last hours of Joy's young life. The doctors were drawing with a black magic marker on Joy's legs to keep track of the size of the marks. Were they increasing in size? Was she still hemorrhaging? The answer was yes. Her body was still hemorrhaging and her blood was clotting at the same time. Her pain was excruciating because of the swelling in her legs, which had swollen to more than twice their size. The fluid in them was stretching the skin so tightly it appeared the skin would burst open at any minute.

Time was passing and the doctors were doing everything they could to fight this virus. However, since a virus has to run its course, little can be done to change its course. Nevertheless, with all that Joy was enduring, she was still clinging to life. She did not appear frightened. Her breathing was regular, deep and even and so we too consciously maintained a calm demeanor for her sake. As shocked and terrified as we were, I sensed that Joy would react as we did. If we acted out of control, she would become anxious as well. If we appeared confident, she would sense our peace. We knew that Joy's future was out of the hands of the doctors and out of our hands as well. The decision concerning her life was going to come down from above.

Dr. Poncz reported to us regularly about what was happening, what to expect, and what his team of doctors were attempting to do to reverse the course of Joy's virus. Ken and I knew we were at the mercy of God and these doctors. Although we had never been in this hospital before, we were fully aware of its world-renowned reputation as an outstanding children's hospital with excellent doctors and nurses. We had certainly read about some of the miracles that had happened here for other children with special needs. We knew if there was hope for Joy to live, we were in the right place. And we were fully aware, even now, that it would take a miracle.

The minutes and hours passed. Ken and Tina and I were in Joy's room spending as much time with her as possible, fully aware that the clock was ticking and that it only had 12 hours on it. I leaned over and gently stroked her hair, tenderly touching her small face and telling her how much I loved her. Ken held her hand and gazed into her eyes lovingly. Words did not come to him right now. Tina was assuring her that we were all here with her and that we were going to stay with her.

Although we were unaware of the scientific and medical reasons for what the doctors proposed to try, we were grateful and supportive of their ideas. We were willing to try anything. Why not? What did we have to lose? A medication that thins the blood called heparin was given to her and hopefully would stop the clotting that was going on in her body. Blood tests were being taken regularly so doctors could keep an eye on how aggressively the disease was behaving, and they could get information on how effective their methods were at controlling and defeating this disease. Joy was also given a complete blood exchange in hopes that the new uninfected blood would either dilute the life threatening activity or halt it altogether. Heroic measures were indeed being taken to save her life. However calm I looked, inside I was screaming in pain from a broken heart and the fear of losing my child forever.

Each moment of life gave us hope for more. Although we were in the room with her as much as possible, it became difficult to converse with her because she was receiving morphine for the pain that put her into a state of drowsiness. However, she was pain free which was very important to me. I did not want my child to suffer. The important thing was that she was still alive and that meant something to everyone. Clearly, no one was willing to give up hope.

Miraculously, Joy survived the 12 hours. Next the doctors had to consider a plan to continue to support her life. Since the swelling in her legs was cutting off the circulation to her feet, they were turning black. We now became aware of another team of doctors headed by Dr. John Templeton, a surgeon, who told us that a surgical procedure was necessary to relieve the pressure on her legs. Her legs would be sliced open so that the blood supply could get to the muscle in an attempt to save her legs. However, the heparin, a blood thinner, had to be stopped so that she did not bleed to death during the surgical procedure. We wondered what would happen if the heparin, which seemed to be helping her, was stopped. On the other hand, what would happen if she did not have the procedure to relieve the pressure in her legs? No one knew for certain which choice was the absolute right one, but, if life was ahead for Joy, we needed to decide as best we could with the information we had, and we had to trust God and the doctors. We made the decision to stop the heparin and go ahead with the procedure.

The procedure was a success. However, when we saw Joy after the procedure, we were horrified at the appearance of her legs!

Already my little girl's legs were almost twice their original size from swelling and black and blue from hemorrhaging, and her toes had shriveled up and were black. Now, to add to all of that, the surgeons split her legs from the knee down to just above the ankle in about six places on each leg, the flesh itself just flopped open, and the muscle was completely exposed. Each leg looked like a piece of meat gone bad and someone had tried to save what little good meat was still left by cutting away the bad meat with a very sharp knife. Intellectually I knew that these procedures had to be done if we were to win the battle against this virus and now the bacteria, but I had to remind myself that somewhere in this nightmare was my little girl.

Although Joy's legs did not physically resemble themselves any longer, she was still alive. Time was on our side now. Though her surviving this crisis gave us hope, we never felt completely out of the woods in the entire ordeal. We only felt that we had achieved small victories over the unseen enemy, the virus and its terrible path of destruction.

Chapter Eight

Lifesaving Procedures: Debriedements

Now that Joy's legs were split open, bacteria became the new enemy. Since the skin and tissue were dying on her legs and she did not have skin covering her legs, the whole area became the breeding ground for bacteria. Joy was taken into surgery every day and sometimes twice a day for a procedure called debreidement. Bacteria were rapidly eating away at her body and had to be removed before they could overpower the body and cause her death. Debriedement is a surgical process that requires the patient to be taken into the operating room and given anesthesia. Then the surgeon, using a surgical knife, cuts away or scrapes away the sections of the skin and tissue that are infected with the bacteria in an attempt to remove the bacteria. Bleeding during and following this procedure indicates that the bacteria have been removed and there is good healthy tissue remaining. However, since there was no skin covering Joy's legs, the bacteria quickly came back and the whole process began again.

Dr. Templeton was as committed to the process of saving Joy's life and limbs as we were. He was an extremely focused individual. Every day — sometimes twice a day, he took her into the OR (operating room) for this debriedement procedure. Each time Joy would recover from surgery and the next plan for her care would be made, he was there. Joy's care did not stop on the weekends. Her care had to be 24 hours a day and seven days a week and it seemed that Dr. Templeton was always there. As a physician, he could intelligently calculate her chances of survival and the real probability of her legs surviving. However, his focus was to keep her legs alive. Saving her legs, of course, was secondary to saving her life. But in the event that she made it, he was determined that her physical body was going to be as much intact and able to support her life as possible. Great pains were being taken to save those legs with the desperate hope that she would walk again someday.

Dr. Templeton never seemed overwhelmed or without hope, no matter what was going on. He was quite a man: an unusually dedicated physician, extremely talented and skilled in his medical specialty, extraordinary in meeting the challenge of unusual situations with confidence, and equally determined to achieve a positive outcome no matter what the odds appeared to be. He was deliberate in his thinking, talking and actions and never, in our experience, appeared to be without absolute focus and without a willingness to overcome the impossible. We did not know anything about this doctor before this tragic situation occurred. We did not have time to select a surgeon. We do not know why or how he became Joy's doctor, but we would forever be grateful to him and to God for selecting Dr. John Templeton as Joy's surgeon.

Another Dr. Templeton who was vital to Joy's care and surgical procedures was Josephine (Dr. Pina) Templeton, an anesthesiologist, who was married to Dr. John Templeton. In the OR itself a team of people were being put in place to make this horrifying and traumatizing situation the best it could possibly be this side of heaven. As Joy continued to have daily surgical procedures, Dr. Pina recognized Joy's anxiety mounting as she waited in the OR holding area for her turn to go into surgery. Being a sensitive and caring physician and a mother herself, Dr. Pina suggested that Joy could begin to be "relaxed" in her room to eliminate some of her anxiety. Dr. Pina Templeton then came to Joy's hospital room and began the process of "relaxing" her medically by administering a drug to begin calming her before she reached the OR. The Templetons' dedication to their patient did not stop there. Both doctors came into the hospital on their days and weekends off to personally continue Joy's debreidement procedures. The consistency in her care was vital to the outcome. Their personal sacrifice was enormous. They were unbelievably devoted to both the situation and to Joy personally.

Many, many extra measures of compassion were extended to Joy. Another dedicated individual was Dot Cohen, a seasoned veteran of the transport team. Her job was to wheel a patient on a stretcher to a holding area outside the operating room to wait for surgery. Then after surgery, she would take the patient back to the room or to the ICU (most likely the place where Joy would be going). Dot, too, could see the anxiety mounting in Joy each time she would go to get her for surgery. Dot volunteered to be the person who would go for Joy every time, so that Joy could see a friendly and familiar face and at least be comforted in that. Dot also came in on her days off to keep consistency in the process.

Joy, cranky and weary of all her procedures, sometimes greeted anyone who arrived with a stretcher to take her to surgery with shouts of "Go away!" "Leave me alone!" Knowing that Joy was just weary of the everyday procedures, Dot made the effort to make it a little easier for Joy. Dot knew that anyone taking care of Joy needed a big heart and a strong will and Dot herself was certainly one of these people. I can still hear her shout, "Keep your hands off my stretcher!" to anyone attempting to help her guide "her" stretcher with Joy aboard, through the halls, around corners and on and off the elevators. She let everyone within earshot know she had things under control and that there was precious cargo on her stretcher.

The constant medical procedures were vitally necessary to keep Joy alive, but it was heart warming for me to know that so many people went the extra mile to provide as much human concern for her as well. I can only imagine how the OR team and OR nurses felt each time this child came in for a procedure. They always acted so upbeat, but their eyes could not hide their tremendous empathy for this little girl who once again was going into the OR for either surgery or a procedure. Each day they knew that once again, Joy was going to be mutilated, purposefully and with absolute necessity to save her life and limbs. It was both horrifying and extremely difficult to be a part of such a gruesome process. Every moment presented a challenge and a threat and never for one minute were we ever assured of her survival.

Chapter Nine

Living in the Hospital

Day after day Joy would go into surgery for debriedement which meant she rarely ate or drank because she was always being readied for surgery or just coming out. Daily removal of the bacteria on her legs was crucial if her life was to be saved. However, Joy often craved something to eat and thirsted after a drop of water but both were strictly forbidden before surgery. She would become annoyed when she was in the holding area of the operating room and would imagine she smelled food. She felt sure the holding room was just above the cafeteria, even though it was not. But her stern food restrictions made her crave food, which was one more frustration for her.

Imagine getting mind and psyche ready for surgery **every** day. First, patients preparing for surgery are understandably anxious about the procedure, then the results, then the pain, then the recuperation and recovery. Often they are very concerned that they cannot eat or drink for a specific period of time. I marveled that Joy bravely faced these fears and frustrations every day.

When she could eat, we would accommodate her choices of food as best we could. Various family members even went into the city, Philadelphia, to get her cheesesteaks, spaghetti and Chinese food. McDonald's, located on the first floor of the hospital, sold hamburgers and French fries, her favorite food. Joy became known around the hospital for her ability to eat almost immediately after surgery. The minute she was "recovered" she wanted to eat.

Throughout all of this, Ken and I were living at Children's Hospital. At CHOP, there was a room for the parents of children in the Intensive Care Units. Parents could pull up two chairs to sleep on, or, if they were lucky, they could get the chairs that converted to a bed or maybe the rollaway that was in the side room. The children in this area were seriously ill and their parents camped out in this room, anticipating some good news. Generally the parents would come and go as their children would improve and would then be sent to another floor to completely recover. The parents then would go to the other patient floor as well. Eventually, the family would return home to their daily lives and routines. But not all children got better and went home, and we were still not sure what would happen to Joy.

Tina was staying with my brother and his wife until school ended for the summer. She would join us in the evening if someone who was coming to the hospital could bring her, and on the weekends she would "live" with us at the hospital. Because of our businesses, our children were used to sharing both their space and their lives with other people.

Weeks passed, and Ken and I had not gone home or to work. My sister would bring us clean clothes, take the dirty ones home, and repeat the process as often as we needed it. Our wonderful managers and employees were running our businesses — two hairstyling salons and the drycleaners. The clients, too, were dedicated, concerned and supportive.

The company from whom I purchased my beauty supplies, East Coast Salon Services, continued to supply the salons with products to keep them running regardless of the bill or its non-payment. Ken and I were privileged to enjoy a very special friendship with the two principals of East Coast Salon Services and their wives, Stan and Cora Klet and Joe and Marianna Marcelli. As personal friends and business friends, they empathized with our circumstances and facilitated a plan to safeguard our livelihood until we could get back on our feet and provide for our family when this crisis was over. Our East Coast salesman, Michael Silverman, became instrumental in helping place the weekly supply order, which was vital to keeping the salons operating.

And, by the way, we had no money to live on. We were not working and yet we had expenses. We were eating every meal in the hospital. To make matters worse, we had no health insurance. We had just dropped ours in anticipation of getting new coverage. Imagine the debt that was mounting. Nevertheless, when I saw that Joy had the will to live, I was willing to give up everything to bring my little girl home. I totally detached from every material thing I had and was willing to sacrifice everything we had for her. If Joy could not walk away from the trauma and devastation, the surgeries, the pain, the suffering, the visual realization of her body dying right in front of her, then I would not walk away either. We would see this through together to the end, whatever that might be.

One evening as I was sitting in Joy's ICU room, it became obvious to me that a baby (maybe 9 months old) in the next room was not doing well. There were windows between the rooms, and it was easy to see the patient unless the blinds were closed. The night went on and the doctors coming in and out checking on the baby were steady and very solemn. I did not know what was wrong with the child, but I knew his condition was serious and grave. It was so sad to realize that this little soul might not be there in the morning. Why would God choose this little baby's life to end? I did not know the answer to that question. I thought about the sadness his parents were going to endure. Those parents and Ken and I shared something one should never need to experience: the fear of losing a child. Why was Joy still alive and why was this baby going to die? The reason for the death of this innocent baby was inconceivable; yet, God determined that the end of his life was to be on this particular day. Before morning the baby passed away. Ken and I witnessed firsthand that children do die.

I was reminded of the death of my good friend from church when she was 19 and I was 21. She was in an automobile accident and died. There was not a scratch on her. Had she been frightened to death? The pastor who spoke at her funeral said that sometimes God takes people out of this world because something very tragic is going to happen to them and He prevents it. How kind of Him. How sad for us. It was difficult to understand her death. Maybe death doesn't always make sense to us. Maybe it shouldn't or we would see it as something we should control.

Realizing that Joy was closer to death than life every second, that her survival beyond this point was still uncertain, I absolutely could not physically move down the hall to the room provided for the parents of these children in ICU.

Even knowing that the room provided a place for us to sit or even sleep, I **could not** go farther down the hall from her room than those wooden benches that lined the corridor outside the ICU. At least from these benches, I could see her as I looked directly into her room through the glass windows that overlooked the atrium. The blinds on these windows were left open unless Joy was having something done to her that required privacy. In those cases, if possible, I would be in the room with her.

So these benches became our home. We slept on them, sat on them, ate on them, visited our family on them, prayed on them and conversed with the doctors on them when we were not in Joy's room. In Joy's Intensive Care room, I slept on the floor next to her bed, leaning on the windowsill, or slumped in a chair. Sleep was NOT eight hours a night. Sleep consisted of only catnaps between Joy's needing or wanting something, or the doctors and nurses coming in to care for her or to get her ready for surgery or to help her recover from surgery. Usually anyone in the hospital could find Ken and me camped out on the benches.

We spent 24 hours a day with Joy; awake most of the time, eating from a paper tray from the cafeteria or a paper bag from McDonald's. We showered in the shower rooms that the hospital provided for parents who were spending the night. I don't suppose when the hospital was designed, anyone planned on parents being there around the clock for months on end. I only now can appreciate the hospital's concern for our family living in the corridor on the fourth floor. How odd it must have looked, but to us, it was natural for us to be near her. We would move from one end of the corridor where I could see into her room to the other end where the operating room was located. Periodically, Grace Gadston from the social work department would come visit us and suggest that we go home at night. "Get a break," she would say, or "Why not stay at the Ronald McDonald house in the city?" She was concerned for us — rightfully so. BUT I physically could not go that far away from Joy. I feared that an emergency would arise any moment, which it often did.

One night, after we had spent weeks living in the hospital, Ken and I agreed to stay in the hotel across the street from the hospital to get some rest. He was the first to get up and go into the hospital. Once in Joy's room, he noticed that the same spidery black marks that had been on her legs were now surrounding her left elbow. We knew that her legs might not survive and could be amputated, but now an arm? This new twist was TOO MUCH, and this frightening development happened when we were not there. I couldn't handle not being there, so back to the benches we went. I finally figured out how to get some rest during the day. Since I was living on catnaps and could not sleep during the day very well, I had to find a place to rest. With Joy going into surgery every day, I discovered I had at least two somewhat predictable hours. Joy's surgeries gave me the longest period of time in the day and night without interruption. I chose to use these two hours to sleep in the back seat of our car which we had left in the parking garage under the hospital. Our car became a welcomed refuge!

Chapter Ten

Hospital Wardrobe

Along with adjusting to the "living" conditions within the hospital, we needed to dress for the occasion, requiring a different type of wardrobe. Both Ken and I needed clothes we could sleep in and live in, because we could be in the same clothes for 12-24 hours or more. It was also 1982 when "sweats" and sneakers and this ultra-casual type of clothing were not as available as they are now. The clothes and shoes we wore needed to be both comfortable and respectable looking, as we were sleeping around other people who were working. Therefore I dressed in sweat pants or jeans and a sweatshirt with a T-shirt underneath so I could remove the sweatshirt if it became too warm. Ken generally dressed in jeans and a wash and wear cotton shirt adding a sweatshirt as needed.

Since things happened quickly and unexpectedly, I did not feel I had the luxury of taking the time to change my clothes. I certainly did not feel we could or should be in nightwear. Therefore, I slept and lived in the same clothes, never even removing my shoes for fear something would happen and I wouldn't have time to put them back on. I always wore sneakers and socks, as they were comfortable to walk in and okay to sleep in. My sister volunteered to go shopping to get the clothes we needed and also continued picking up our dirty garments and replacing them with clean clothes each time she came to visit. Now as I reflect back on this time, I realize I was living like a soldier in a war zone who needed to be ready at all times. In the years to come, I would always have my own hospital wardrobe on hand and ready to go.

Ken and I made new friends at the hospital. Since we were there around the clock for months, we had the opportunity to meet many people. What beloved friends they became, as this was now our home away from home.

Tina, now 11, was tremendously heroic. After school ended for the year, she went to stay with her relatives, Jack and Joanne Fowler and their six children, in Delano, Pennsylvania. These people are the most loving and caring people imaginable along with being a family of faith and discipline. I was more than comfortable with Tina being with them although she was farther away from the hospital and us. Tina affectionately referred to them as Aunt Joanne and Uncle Jack. Joanne is angelic in her love and compassion towards everyone. She is blessed with a gift of hospitality and welcomes everyone into her home with a big heart and her specialty, a beef roast in the oven. Her husband, my cousin Jack, is the disciplinarian. When he told any of his children they were not to do something, he meant it and they knew it.

One day Jack told Tina she was not to hang out at a firehouse a few blocks from their home where young men were accustomed to gathering. Well, it looked like a great spot to be, so Tina went there. Soon one of her younger cousins, Jack's son, was sent to bring her home. Reluctantly, Tina went back to the house. Once again, but more firmly, Jack told her that she was not to go there or he would "beat her bottom." Tina immediately warned him that if he hit her, she would call her Dad and tell him that Jack had disciplined her. Tina felt certain that her Dad would jump right in the car and drive to Delano both to rescue his beloved daughter, Tina, and to reprimand

Jack. Without missing a beat and obviously unshaken by Tina's threat, Jack promptly retorted, "Maybe you should call him now and by the time he gets here your spanking will be over". That ended that. Tina did not go to the firehouse again. Jack and Joanne raised six children, all very wonderful people, in a loving, compassionate home centered on God's principles (and with a little of the Mahanoy City Elks' influence) with a strong hand and a warm heart.

We also made every effort to maintain our family's unit while we were living in the hospital. We looked forward to returning home not completely devastated, but somewhat intact. I strongly feel that since we were with her, Joy was encouraged to fight. This war was not just hers to fight. We were all committed to it. We were the constant in this scenario. Many things in our lives were changing: where we lived, how we lived, when and what we ate, where we slept, if we slept, our financial security, our plans for our future as a family, even our friends were changing. Some of our friends became even more important in our lives as they joined our battle. The thing that did not change was our family. We stayed together and stuck together, each realizing the sacrifice being made was to save a life — Joy's.

Chapter Eleven

Understanding a Teaching Hospital

In a teaching hospital there are many, many people around at all times. Since CHOP was a teaching hospital and learning was certainly an important part of the agenda, Joy was a medical mystery everyone wanted to see and talk to. Besides the doctors on her medical services team, many other doctors, interns and residents from almost every medical specialty came to visit her.

In addition to the attentiveness of doctors, I can't begin to tell you about the love and compassion and dedication of the nurses. They not only took care of Joy's physical needs, but also were very much in tune with our needs as a family and Joy's as a little girl. Because so much was happening to her all the time, the nurses suggested that there should be times when nothing would be done to her: no blood drawn, no x-rays, no intrusions or intruders of any kind. This would be the time the play therapist would come spend time with Joy. Joy could be a child again. The opportunity to be young and carefree and to play like any other child had been taken from Joy because of her condition and need for medical attention and procedures, but the nurses and play therapists knew that she needed time set aside to be a little girl too, and they made it happen for her.

It was interesting to me as well that the nurses on the patient floors were very authoritative and very much in control of their patients.

Since it was a teaching hospital, the residents who rotated through every three months were constantly changing. The nurses respected their position as doctors, yet realized that the residents would be here for only three months and their patients may have been on the floor before the residents began their rotation at CHOP and possibly would still be there after they left. The nurses knew their patients and were very protective of them, so it appeared that the nurses needed to approve whatever medications or treatments the residents ordered before the medications or treatments would be implemented. The nurses were very diplomatic, but I certainly knew who was in charge on the floors. Those nurses knew how to guide the newer residents to the right decisions, or they knew when to bring the chief resident, fellow, or the attending physician into the process.

One thing we needed to learn in a teaching hospital was which doctor to ask questions of. The benefits of being in a teaching hospital are many. The downside, however, should also be understood. The first year resident is referred to as "doctor" but has just finished medical school. This doctor could be doing a three-month rotation through the hospital for general training. Residency programs can last up to five years. A "chief resident" is usually a resident who is in the last year of the residency program and has been chosen to be in charge of the other residents on a specific service such as internal medicine or general surgery. A fellow is a resident who is specializing in a certain specialty of medicine such as cardiology, infectious disease or orthopedic surgery and has already completed a general residency program. The fellow's authority falls just below the attending physician's and the fellow's knowledge of a specific area of medicine is usually greater than a resident's. In Joy's unusual case, it was especially important to direct our concerns to an attending physician, a fellow or a chief resident who had the necessary experience and authority to make decisions.

The residents sometimes were as helpful as they could be, extremely compassionate, earnest in their desire to be professionals, but a bit inexperienced. This was a problem in Joy's extraordinary case. Although I truly enjoyed meeting them and some became life -long friends, I needed to know which doctors had the experience and knowledge to make a difference in Joy's care. I would ask new doctors upon our first meeting, "And what year resident are you?" I always politely answered all their questions concerning Joy because I realized they were very interested and that part of their training was to get to know the patient and to collect information for the patient's record.

We made friends with many of the residents because, like us, they were at the hospital seven days a week and 24 hours a day. Once, when Joy was in a stable condition, Ken and I were invited to have dinner in Philadelphia at the apartment of one of the surgical residents and her fiancé who was a resident at another Philadelphia hospital.

I even began cutting hair for many of the residents at strange hours of the night because we were all awake anyway. It was amusing to me that once I started cutting their hair, they each became the typical client, sharing their thoughts and their lives with me. Many of the residents that Ken and I had befriended left after their rotation was over at CHOP, unfortunately never knowing if Joy had survived.

Chapter Twelve

Hope Changes

Joy was finally moved into a regular patient room after about three weeks in the Intensive Care Unit. The virus was no longer active, was no longer a threat, and Joy was no longer contagious. On this patients' floor, the hospital had a banana boat, a wooden "boat" on wheels shaped like a gondola with a long handle attached in the back to push it.

For the first time since arriving at the hospital on May 2, Joy could be lifted out of her bed and into this banana boat. It was a thrilling moment for us as we pushed her up and down the corridor. We were every bit as thrilled as any parents who displayed their beautiful children in a parade. Yet Joy, who at one time was a cute blonde-haired little girl, was now far from that person. She had lost most of her hair due to trauma and poor nutrition, even though she was being fed intravenously. Even her face was quite different in shape. It was round from the steroids she was taking. She looked very ill, medicated and sad. Yet this stroll down the corridor gave us some glimmer of hope. It was our first moment of triumph and we were thrilled to be pushing our daughter down the corridor in the "banana boat".

Once Joy moved into a regular hospital room, we became a bit more hopeful for her survival. We had begun to measure hope in different ways. For instance, in the beginning we hoped Joy's was just a simple case of chicken pox. Then, we hoped the marks on her legs meant nothing. Then, when she went to the hospital, we hoped the doctors could do something to help her. Next, we hoped the doctors could save her from this disease that we had never heard about and whose prognosis was grim. We hoped the doctors were doing all they could to save her life. Finally we had the simple hope that she would someday get out of the hospital bed and into that banana boat. And it was a glorious day when she did.

A week after the joyous banana boat ride was June 2, and Joy turned seven. The hospital provided a birthday cake and a party of sorts in the play room on the 6th floor where children would go to play and try to forget about their reasons for being in the hospital. We made our greatest efforts to be light hearted and cheerful, desiring to celebrate Joy's special day with her. A typical question of the birthday girl was asked by my mother, "Joy, are you having a happy birthday?" Joy too had been trying hard to act like a seven-year-old on her birthday, excited and enthusiastic for the occasion, but Mom's question brought her back to reality. Joy responded sadly with, "Grandmom, would you be happy today if you were in this bed?"

Chapter Thirteen

A New Standard of Normal

Living in a patient's room was like living in a dormitory. There were five other children along with their parents in this room. We seemed very different from the other parents in the room and to me it was very obvious why. The other parents were talking about their children getting better and going home soon, while we were just beginning to settle into our new living quarters, this hospital room. We had no immediate plans to go home and we still did not know for sure that Joy was going to get better.

Since I am a person who likes space and privacy, living with all these people was another adjustment I had to make. I wondered if I would ever be the same person after this. Would any of us? We were evolving into people with little resemblance to the people we had been before because, in order to survive, we were assimilating into our environment.

We tried to make the best of our situation by becoming the host family of the room, explaining to the newly arriving children and their parents where they could find the cafeteria, blankets, cots, the parents' shower and other useful information. Our openness brought about a wonderful opportunity to get to know these parents and their children and talk to them about what was going on outside the hospital — a life we had not been a part of for a few weeks. The parents shared humorous stories of recent adventures of their children and other funny incidents that took place in their families and we all laughed. It felt so good to laugh.

One couple we met had a daughter who was going to be in the hospital for a long period of time, so we gravitated toward them and shared that misfortune. I eat under stress, but Ken couldn't eat. The little girl's father suffered from the same need to eat as I, so we would all go down stairs to McDonalds and the father and I would order hamburgers and ice cream sundaes to eat while his wife and Ken would go outside to smoke and then would join us for their usual cup of coffee. Each of us was trying to manage our stress as best we could.

The medical problems of the children in this room and on this patient floor did not appear to be as serious as Joy's. But how insensitive of me to believe that our situation and suffering could be greater than anyone else was experiencing! Joy had recently left the ICU where serious and life-threatening conditions existed and I had no idea that death could be on this floor for these children as well.

However, one day I looked down the hall and saw a room with all the blinds closed. I enjoyed looking out the window into the hall and seeing the people smiling and laughing as they went about their normal activities. As I watched, I saw a girl about ten years old who appeared reasonably healthy, walk with her mother into a patient's room adjacent to Joy's room. Doing a little detective work on my own, I found out that the young girl had cystic fibrosis. Her time had come and she was not expected to live past the weekend. This information is not generally discussed as it is private, but living in the hospital allowed us to acquire bits of information. I found this young girl's imminent death hard to believe since she literally walked into the room unaided. The days went by and the blinds remained closed. Her parents were by her side all the time. As the weekend approached, I thought for sure the prognosis had to be wrong. I was anticipating her coming out of that room walking hand in hand with her mother as she had entered it just a brief time ago. But then the stretcher came. The little girl was laid upon it and was taken somewhere else in the hospital. And the blinds were opened once again. As was the natural course for this horrible disease, the little girl had indeed passed away.

The death of this little girl was so, so sad, yet an eye opener and a reminder that children do die, even on this floor, and so could Joy. I wanted to pray, but it was difficult to actually pray today. I just couldn't find the words to say. In truth, I had a sense that there was no need to start praying because I had never really stopped praying. Even though I was not uttering words, I felt as though I was in a constant prayerful state where God was listening and answering my prayers. I no longer had a "normal" life, but was living in accord with God where time and life had different meanings, and where things beyond human comprehension and miracles were happening routinely.

In a way, I guess, things were normal for us — surgery was still every day. Joy was still not able to eat. We were still living in the hospital. And Dr. Templeton still came out to speak to us every time after surgery. This became our new standard of normal.

Chapter Fourteen

Talk of Amputation

The threat of the virus had passed, but its destruction to the body still had to be dealt with for Joy to have any future. With increasing dread, I noticed that the lower part of her right leg was totally black. Her toes were shriveled up like raisins.

A new group of doctors was introduced to us, the orthopedic surgeons, Dr. Hugh Watts and Dr. Ronald Ellis. After asking to speak to us privately, Dr. Watts gently began, "I'm sure you can see that Joy will never walk on this diseased leg. In fact, her leg is now considered gangrenous. Something has to be done before she goes septic, which happens when the bacteria generally invades the body. Sepsis is life threatening."

"He's going to mention an amputation," I thought as my mind raced ahead of his explanation. Hoping against the obvious, I braced myself for his next words.

Dr. Watts continued, "Presently we can observe the condition of Joy's lower right leg to be composed of dead tissue, skin and muscle. As you can see, the skin on her lower right leg is black from lack of circulation or blood supply to the extremity, and, for the same reason, her foot is black and her toes are shriveled. However, at this point, the left leg, though still questionable as to its future function, does not appear as diseased."

I held my breath, terrified at what I knew he would say next.

Dr. Watts continued, "Over time the body will demarcate itself to let us know where the amputation should occur. It is prudent to make the decision at the appropriate time, so for now we will just watch and wait."

With the daily situation consuming all my energy and time, I hadn't actually processed the concept of Joy's leg being amputated. It was clear that her leg was dead; but to agree to cutting it off — I wasn't there yet and didn't know if I ever could be in agreement with amputation. Trying desperately to comprehend this new and frightening prospect, I consoled myself that at least she would have one leg remaining. Even if the toes had to be removed, she would still have her other leg and her other foot.

Obediently and fearfully waiting for the signal that the time had arrived for the amputation, Ken and I were still experiencing every day, along with Joy, her level of discomfort. Joy's pain was excruciating, even though she was on a constant morphine drip with boluses of additional medication as needed. Occasionally her IV lines would "blow," which meant the vein into which the IV went would no longer accept the medication or any intravenous fluids and a new IV had to be started. Eventually those needle pricks became intolerable, so Joy had a central line surgically put in while she was in the OR. This central line eased some of Joy's suffering by allowing anyone who needed to draw blood and to administer certain medications to do so without a new needle prick each time.

The nursing staff had regular meetings to discuss Joy's comfort and what they could do to make Joy's life resemble the life of a normal seven year old. They were searching for ways to help Joy be a little girl while this experience was making her both wise and mature beyond her years. The nurses never lost sight of the fact that she was a person with normal feelings. For instance, because of her daily surgeries, she was always in a hospital gown. It was easier for her not to be wearing underwear, but she INSISTED on wearing underpants! Because of her heavily bandaged legs, she could not put underpants on herself or take them down when she needed to use the bedpan, which complicated things, but this was one thing she absolutely insisted on. So we all complied with her wishes… even to the point that immediately after surgery, the recovery room nurses would put her underpants on for her as soon as it was possible. She was treated with respect in the demands that could be permitted even if it made the nurses' jobs a little more difficult. They were amazing in their willingness to care for the whole person.

I helped take care of Joy on a day-to-day basis. I would wash her and tend to her as much as I could without interfering with the medical attention she needed. This accomplished many things. It gave me the sense of mothering my child in the only way I still could. It gave Joy the sense that I was still involved with her as a mother, that she wasn't turned over to someone else for everything. It kept our bond in place. Also, I felt that if I did all the little things for Joy, like bathing her, brushing her teeth, getting her food and drinks, and changing her bed, this would give the nurses a break. Joy had tremendous needs and any nurse assigned to her on any shift had a big job. As a result of my help for the routine things, when we did make a request, mostly for pain medication or something of a serious nature, the nurses knew it was an urgent request and they would respond quickly.

I became very familiar with the kitchen on each floor where additional food was stored for the patients. When Joy wanted a treat and was permitted to eat, we would go to the kitchen and get small containers of milk and individual cups of ice cream to make her a milk shake. We would put the ingredients into a baby bottle and shake and shake until we produced what resembled a milk shake.

It helped to soften the ice cream in the microwave first. This was fun and it gave us something enjoyable we could do together as a family. And homemade milk shakes sure tasted good, especially to Joy, who hardly ever had the opportunity to eat. It was also a little exhilarating to be eating ice cream anytime of the day or night. We would smirk and snicker a little under our breath because drinking milkshakes at forbidden times was a little mischievous. But things were different for us now, and anytime was a good time for her to be able to enjoy the taste of something good. After all, her basic nutritional needs were being met through the liquid diet supplement she was receiving through her IV.

Along with being one of the master milkshake makers, I became Joy's advocate, a word I didn't even know at the time. Since I was with her around the clock, I became the clearinghouse for the most current information on Joy. I so appreciated the way the hospital's doctors, nurses and other staff regarded me personally. They included me in the information and in the decision making for her as was appropriate. I remember one day being in the playroom with Joy when a new resident came in to get her history. There was a new rotation of residents and their job was to get to know the patient's history and needs. When the new resident began asking me questions about Joy, I began to answer. Then he started to ask detailed medical questions about Joy using medical terminology. Although I felt as though I could answer his technical questions, it occurred to me that he might have thought I was her nurse. So I said to him, "You should know that I am only her mother." "Oh, I know that," he replied, "but the word is, that if you want to know anything pertaining to Joy, you're the one to ask." Somehow I had won the doctors' trust and was very grateful.

It was difficult being a part of the team caring for her, being on top of the medications, the present condition, her needs and changes in her mental or physical condition, listening to and absorbing information, learning the medical jargon, staying in the role of being her mother and keeping up to speed with learning what was happening, but it was necessary for me. Although this hospital and the doctors and nurses were extremely competent, Ken and I had to understand and agree with what was happening, what was planned and what was going to be done to her. Because of our special bond, I knew I was to be the one to whom Joy would turn to help her sort out, in her young mind, each procedure that was happening to her and I had to know how to answer her questions to give her the peace and comfort that she so needed. I could not say to her "I do not know." I needed to be a player on the team even if I was only carrying the water.

Fortunately, God gave me an ability to recall what I had just heard. So when one team of doctors would come in to discuss Joy's progress or non-progress, and then the next group would come in, and the next group of nurses or social workers, I could retain what they were all saying, process it, and often relay it to the next group who needed to know what the last group had to say. This was the most important time of my life and I had to engage all of my abilities and keep them working, because every detail could improve or compromise her life. With God's help, I was able to understand and consent with her treatment and surgeries even when the worst came. I only had one patient to care for and to focus on and the doctors and nurses had many. I needed to be an expert on this patient, my daughter.

Chapter Fifteen

God's Promise

Dr. Watts asked to talk to Ken and me privately after Joy's procedure late in the afternoon on a Thursday. It had only been a week since our last serious conversation with Dr. Watts and Ken and I suspected we knew what he wanted to discuss with us. Dr. Watts once again reaffirmed what we already knew: Joy's right leg was seriously diseased, damaged, and decayed and it needed to be amputated. Although I knew this intellectually, this was my little girl we were discussing. The amputation was difficult to accept, yet there was no other alternative. I knew that. Her left leg was not as bad and the determination could not and should not be made yet about that leg. Joy was scheduled for the amputation of her right leg the next morning early, first case.

My heart was heavy. Joy had already been through so much and now this. We knew that this was coming, but now it was here. It seemed that all energy immediately left my body. At this moment I could not be anything but the mother of this little girl. Tomorrow she would have one leg. Her life would completely change if she lived. What would it be like? How would she get around? Her leg was seriously decayed and the debriedements removed all of the skin on the leg up into the upper thigh, as well as much of the subcutaneous tissue just below the skin. Joy's leg already did not look like something a person could walk on, and now it would become just a stump with no foot. This was a new low for me. How would she live her life?

We walked back to Joy's room along with Dr. Watts, so that he could tell her what was going to happen in the morning. It was now early evening. It was an extremely solemn moment for all of us. After Dr. Watts left, Joy turned to me and pleaded, "Mommy, don't let them cut off my leg. Why are YOU letting them cut off my leg?"

I had no answers, but tried to comfort her as best I could. I was so totally inadequate at this moment. I needed to give comfort, encouragement and hope to Joy, but I didn't yet have them to give. As best I could, I tried to calm her, distract her and get her to sleep. The transport team was coming to take her to the operating room at 5:30 in the morning. Ken slept at the foot of her bed on a cot and I at the side of her bed on another. We all tossed and turned and were extremely restless. We were trying not to awaken the other children and parents in the room. At some time throughout the night, I whispered to Ken, " I will be right back." There was no further explanation needed and none asked for. We were all still absorbing the reality of Joy having her leg amputated in the morning.

I went downstairs to the hospital chapel, a non-denominational chapel carved out of a corner in the back hall on the first floor, adorned with modern stained glass windows in a semi-circle near the entrance, a simple altar and a few chairs. It was, most importantly, the place to talk to God. I didn't sit in His presence. I knelt on the floor with my hands folded supporting my bowed head leaning on a chair. I was distraught. Through my anguish I prayed from my broken heart:

"*Father, please, please help us!*
I know You know what is going to happen, but I am so scared
and uncertain about tomorrow's surgery!
Will she be all right?
What will her life be like with only one leg?
Will she really be okay?
I have no words of comfort for her, Father.
I don't understand so much of what is happening to her.
I love her so much and I want her to live, but not just for my
sake, but because You see a life for her after this is over.
This is beyond me and I feel empty of words
to give her hope and encouragement.
I am filled with despair.
I know that this is the right thing medically to do; yet I do not
know that the future will be okay or that she will be okay. I do
not know these things. I am brokenhearted!
You said, "I will never leave you nor forsake you."
"Ask and it shall be given to you."
I'm asking for Your help.
I know of Your power
and I ask for You to empower the surgeons tomorrow.
Guide them into her body as they make the decision for the
amputation of her leg. Make it just the right spot.
You made her. You know her body.
As the great physician, assist the doctors in this surgery.
From the depths of my heart I ask You to deal with her
directly tonight. Give her the courage I cannot give her, the
comfort I do not feel, the hope I cannot see.
In the name of Your Son, I ask these things,
Amen.

I left the chapel and went back to Joy's room. I shared my request of God with no one. I crawled into bed with Joy and cradled her in my arms. At some point, we both fell asleep. The morning came very quickly. All too soon the transport team would arrive to take her down to the OR for the amputation. As I awakened Joy, I realized that something was very different about her from the night before. She was not anxious. She was not scared. She was not questioning.

I asked her if God had spoken to her last night. With assurance and confidence she replied," YES". I was not surprised, but very, very relieved and grateful. I asked her what God said to her. She responded, "God said, `Joy, you are going to be all right. You will walk and run and play like other kids on false legs'."

God answered my prayer! How could I possibly ever question His love and personal interest in Joy and what was happening to her? Joy never needed to ask who was speaking to her. She knew. This moment changed our whole perspective on what was going to happen to Joy.

First of all, she would live! What a relief!! Hallelujah! Praise God! When God makes a promise, He never changes His mind.

Secondly, God said Joy would walk and run and play like other kids on false LEGS. I now knew what was going to happen to her other leg. It was coming off.

Chapter Sixteen

My God

I was fortunate to be introduced to God at an early age. Let me tell you about my God, the God of creation and the God of our family. He is not just some figment of my imagination and He is not some God someone handed down to me to believe in.

I know what I want in a God. And I know I need One. I am a person who seeks the best professional advice and talents. I search for an extraordinary person who is excellent in his field to employ or engage as best I can afford in every situation. When I need a doctor, I will go anywhere to the best. When I need a carpenter, I find the best. When I need a lawyer, banker, lawn service, house cleaner, I seek out the best. This is because I know there is a difference in the outcome and I spend time finding the best available in the field to do the job I need done.

I want the same in God. I want one who has extraordinary and supernatural abilities to do everything! I want to feel confident that my God will always win in every situation. I need to know that there is not another god more powerful. I need to feel confident that He is always there for me and that He will never fail me. I need to know that He is able to heal a sick and diseased body because He is the great physician. I am not that unusual, talented, or special that I think God would want to spend time with me. Therefore I want a God who does not judge me for my looks, talents, abilities, or inabilities, but Who loves me unconditionally. I also need forgiveness for doing the dumb things I didn't know were wrong and the things I did intentionally that I felt guilty and ashamed of, but did them anyway. And some of these mistakes I may even repeat tomorrow. I want a permanent commitment from God that whatever I do, He will not stop loving me.

I want a God who will interact with me, who will listen to me when I need to talk to Him, and who will show an interest in my life and help me. I want to talk to God whenever I need to — in times of despair, loneliness, hopelessness, happiness, discouragement, depression, sickness, and death, and I want to feel better after talking to Him knowing He heard, will answer, and will make things turn out right. I want a personal God.

I want a God to whom I can tell my secrets. I want Him to know me better than I know myself. I want to be able to cry to Him and not feel embarrassed by my tears. I want to feel His arms around me when I am scared. I need Him to comfort me and show me the way when I feel lost.

I want God to protect my family and me from bad things — there are many bad things going on in this world. I am fully aware there is something other than God's love in this world in which I live. We can refer to these "bad" things any way we choose: evil, hatred, Satan, the devil or just " bad things; but evil does exist and I need to have the assurance that evil will not overcome this world and that my family and loved ones, especially my children and grandchildren, will not be forced to live under the control of this evil. I need to know that the same God who has been there for me will be the same God the day my children and grandchildren need Him.

I need to know that He never changes. I need to feel confident that I can trust God today and every day and that He only wants the best for me and that He will discipline me justly. I want to know and understand death and that I will see my loved ones again in the after life. And I want to live with the confidence that sometime in my existence I will be eternally happy and peaceful.

I have given a great deal of thought to the type of God that I need and want in my life. I have taken the time to learn more about the God of creation and His character, and to put Him to the test on His power and promises and His genuine and sincere interest and love for me. I have found the right God and I may even say the only God who could possibly meet all my needs. His help has guided me through so much pain and uncertainty, and I know I can continue to depend on my God through the rest of my life.

For me, it was an easy decision; I needed God in my life because I needed help with my life. And by the way, He'd love to be your God and help you too!

Chapter Seventeen

Introduction to Prostheses

When Joy was taken to surgery for the amputation of her right leg, Ken and I set out to find the prosthetic department of the hospital which we believed to be in the basement near the physical therapy department. Since God told Joy she would walk again, it was obviously going to be on artificial legs. We didn't know anything about prostheses and couldn't figure out how anyone could actually walk on them. However, Ken and I needed to understand this world of artificial legs and we sought to speak to someone who could explain this phenomenon to us.

I can't describe how surprised I was that I was going to have a disabled child. I had thought that God was so wise not to have given me one at birth because He knew that I would not be very good at raising a special child. Or maybe it was that I was too selfish in my desires and goals to want to give up material comforts to take care of someone who needed me that much. What a lesson this was! I realized that the things I wanted and aspired to obtain did not bring happiness. Ken and I had succeeded to some degree already in our young lives and right now, I could say I thought I was relatively happy because of these successes and the material things they brought. But now, I was willing to give up everything we owned and for which we had worked so hard just to take our daughter Joy home with us.

Our visit with the prosthetist was very enlightening. Jeff, the prosthetist, was very kind and explained how prostheses (artificial limbs) actually work. It was amazing and comforting to know that these devices could hold someone who has lost a leg upright and enable that amputee to walk. Jeff picked up a prosthesis that was currently being made to show us what it looked like and began to use the prosthesis to demonstrate how it was designed. Jeff began by explaining that usually a cast would be taken of the amputee's stump using plaster. From the cast, a mold would be made of the stump, producing a custom socket which would be attached to a pipe and then to a rubber foot. In a below the knee amputation, there would be a pipe from the end of the socket to where the foot is attached. Next there is a strap that wraps around the thigh and over the stump socks The strap is held secure by its Velcro closures. This strap holds the leg in place while the amputee is walking so that the leg does not piston up and down.

"Now, let me explain why stump socks are used," Jeff said as he was taking some stump socks out of a nearby cabinet so that Ken and I could see what they looked like. "These wool stump socks would be pulled onto the stump before placing the stump into the socket. Stump socks are long enough to go over the knee and cover some of the thigh and come in various lengths and weights such as 3-ply and 9-ply. The stump socks are very important because they serve as a barrier and a cushion between the socket and the actual skin on the stump as well as a protection for the skin against the friction that can exist from the stump pistoning in and out of the socket while walking. The stump socks are washed daily and replaced daily for hygienic purposes. The number of socks and the weight of the stump socks can be adjusted daily to accommodate the amputee's comfort level or any swelling in the stump.

"After putting on the desired number and weight of stump socks, the amputees are now ready to put the stump into the socket, strap on the prostheses, stand up, get their balance and walk. In this department, we refer to walking as ambulation."

"It appears to me that it could be very hot inside those legs with all those socks on," I commented.

"It can get pretty hot wearing these prostheses, especially in the summer heat," responded Jeff. "Nevertheless, the socks are necessary."

As Ken and I urged him for more details, Jeff went on to explain, "An amputee tends to perspire more than a non-amputee because their body mass is less since their amputation. However, the body's need to cool down through perspiring has not diminished. This is why many amputees find living in hot, humid weather unbearable and prefer a cooler climate and air conditioning."

Jeff continued educating Ken and me about prostheses saying, "Changes are taking place all the time in our industry and our hope is that the plastics used to mold the legs will become lighter and the coverings that we place over the pipe will make the leg look more natural and appealing, especially to young ladies who wear the legs. In the near future I believe that our industry will develop a better product, enabling the amputee to have an even better quality of life. The many veterans who returned from the Vietnam war as amputees are driving much of the research and development. These veterans are pushing for the type of prosthetic legs and feet that will allow them to resume playing sports and living an active life. Right now, a great deal of research is going on that can make this happen."

Ken and I were begining to feel quite optimistic.

"Now, about the foot," Jeff said, "The type of foot used is very important, because although the feet are made of hard rubber, they are flexible and must bend in order to create a spring action that assists the amputee in accomplishing a normal stepping motion, a gait. Ambulation occurs as one step after another is taken. Because Joy will be a below-the-knee-amputee, walking with the use of prostheses will actually be easy for her because she has her knees."

Jeff then informed Ken and me that Joy would probably need new prostheses about every 9 months because the rest of her body would continue to grow and her artificial legs would need to be changed to keep up with the growth of the rest of her body. Also, the bones in her legs could grow right through the end of the stump because they would not know they were to stop growing at that point. Joy's growth plates still determined her growth, not the amputations. Revisions and further surgery were often necessary in a child. "And," Jeff informed us, "Expect that Joy will also need periodic adjustments to her prostheses because, just like a custom suit, there are nips and tucks needed that make the prostheses fit better."

The statement "easy for Joy to walk on prostheses" did not quite compute to Ken and me because of our very limited knowledge of prostheses. Jeff's words, however foreign and sometimes a bit startling, were nevertheless encouraging. To be told Joy had a chance to walk again, even with prostheses, was enormously uplifting to Ken and me.

Ken and I left thanking Jeff for his willingness to educate us about prostheses, and we acknowledged that we could see the possibility of Joy walking on these artificial legs just as other amputees were doing. But, as happy as we were to embrace this new idea of Joy walking again on prostheses, Ken and I were deeply saddened by the realization that it was only a few weeks ago that Joy walked on her own legs.

Upstairs on the third floor, the surgical procedure that resulted in the amputation of Joy's right leg was over and Joy was returned to her room. In medical terms the operation was a success. Joy's right leg had been amputated about 6 inches below her knee. Since Jeff had explained how much easier it would be for her to walk if she still had her knee(s), we thanked God Joy still had hers. This was yet another example of hope measured on a smaller and different scale. First we hoped she would live. Then we hoped she would not lose her leg. Now we were hopeful of her walking again with that stump because she still had her knee. Our hope continued to change, but we were still hopeful.

Chapter Eighteen

Amputation

Sadness filled Joy's room and the mourning process began for us as a family. Something had died and was no longer with us and that something was Joy's little leg. Joy immediately began peering into the eyes of anyone who came into her room to see if they treated her any differently now that she was "different."

She acted a bit defiant and on guard — ready to defend herself to anyone who dared think of her as handicapped or disabled. She was not ready to be someone else. She was still fighting to be the little girl she knew as Joy. Joy was an opinionated, feisty, determined child and as her mother I now was beginning to appreciate and admire that strong will in her.

Joy soon drifted off to sleep from the anesthesia she had received during the surgery and the pain medication she was now getting for the pain. Bone surgery is very painful and the expectation of the pain being severe had been discussed and planned for even before it became an issue. I was relieved for her comfort. For now, Joy seemed peaceful and as I sat beside her bed holding her hand, I began to unload my heart, filled with both thanksgiving and sorrow, to the Lord:

Lord, thank You for creating Joy to be the person
I have witnessed her to be this day. I know she has the
determination it takes to survive and to fight for what she wants.

*Father, every day when she was getting ready for school, she
would argue with me about what she was going to wear.
Her belligerence and defiance frustrated and infuriated me.
After all, she was only 6 years old, and I thought
she was far too young to exhibit such a strong will.
I had no idea that the bold force I was confronted with
in her every day was Your way of letting me know
that she had the spunk and fortitude to fight this fight
even though she is very young.
Lord, help me see my children as you see them
and as You have purposely created them;
and may I learn to appreciate everything about them,
knowing that you will use it for Your honor and glory.
Right now, Father, I feel a tremendous sorrow, a sorrow
I did not know I would ever experience.
My daughter's leg is gone. It was cut off today.
Lord, I can barely say the words… cut off.*

*Lord, please do not think I am not grateful
that she is still alive.*

*I thank You for that miracle, but Lord,
I still feel a tremendous sadness about her losing her leg.
Lord, as I look into her eyes, there are no tears—I guess because
a soldier does not cry when in a heated battle.*

*Father, does she have to be strong much longer?
Can she ever be a little girl again?
Lord, thank You for those precious comforting words
in the book of Psalms:*

The Lord is my shepherd
I shall not want ...

[I know You will take care of us.]

He maketh me to lie down in green pastures,

[Please give us rest. It will be so difficult for us to sleep tonight with so much on our minds and so much sorrow in our hearts.*]*

He leadeth me beside the still waters....

[You have led Ken and me to still waters today
where we found hope in Joy walking on prostheses.]

He restoreth my soul

[Our faith is in You which brings peace to our soul even in this unfamiliar and frightening place we find ourselves today. Lord, I know You will restore our energies and we will overcome this sorrow.]

He leadeth me in the paths of righteousness for His sake. Yea, though I walk through the valley of the shadow of death, I will fear no evil for Thou art with me ...

[Yes, Lord, we are in the valley of the shadow of death, but we will not be overcome by this storm that engulfs us right now because You are here with us on this day and all the stormy days ahead.]

Lord, thank You for being our Shepherd. Amen.

With all that Joy had gone through, her physical appearance had drastically changed. Before she became ill, she was a slender little girl with a slight build, blonde hair, hazel eyes, a happy face and delicate features. Now, from just poor general health and lying in the bed all the time, she was losing her hair. Joy's face was very round because of the steroid medication she was taking which made her look almost unrecognizable. And now, she had one leg missing and the other with black toes, minus skin and a substantial amount of subcutaneous tissue on both. What a bizarre scene.

However, I saw her through the eyes of love. Hearts have no eyes — only feelings. No matter what she looked like, she was still my little girl and I loved her now more than I ever imagined possible. Wanting children was natural for me and I was more than capable of loving them with all my heart, but this experience made me realize that love was a word that required action, not just a feeling. Even though my original plans and dreams for Joy were changing and there was still so much that I did not know about amputees and what they could actually accomplish on "false legs", I could still envision her and our family sharing times of happiness and realizing that there was a future ahead for us all. I didn't have many opportunities right now to drift off into a dream world, but when I did, I saw smiles on all our faces because we were all home once again. Although there was no clear vision of how her life would unfold, at least there was life ahead.

However strange Joy's physical appearance, this hospital was a place where people really looked beyond the physical to the soul. Joy was still so very alive inside. People couldn't help but get attached to her. Even now at seven years of age, she was to be admired for her courage and perseverance throughout this horrific ordeal and the disfigurement process that was going on. Even though the surgical procedures that caused her disfigurement were saving her life, the reality was that she was physically changing right before our eyes. We all wondered how well she would cope with this. Her nurses were very sensitive to these changes and wanted to help her deal with her new physical appearance.

One of the male nurses who was especially sensitive to Joy's situation bought a girl doll that had a fabric body. He cut off one of the doll's legs. As he was presenting this doll to Joy with great emotion and empathy, he told her a story about this special doll. "You and this doll could become great friends since you have something very special in common," he said. "You both have only one leg." This appeared to be a sensitive psychological approach, he thought, for Joy to share her feelings with this cute doll. Joy was delighted with his thoughtfulness and his compassion. However, she immediately said, "Thank you for the doll, but why did you have to cut her leg off?" Joy seemed to always live in the real world.

Amazingly, even with all that she was going through, she lived in the present. One of the outstanding doctors at CHOP later would remark that he had seen many, many devastating cases involving children and adults. "But," he said, "I have never seen anyone become so disfigured and not go psychotic." This was indeed amazing, but her attitude about herself and her situation was one of acceptance and confidence. As a seven-year-old child, she was teaching all of us the true meaning of faith. After hearing from God, she never once questioned how things were going to turn out. Joy immediately began living her life with confidence. Even through the pain and suffering, the disfigurement, the disappointments and near death experiences, Joy knew that life was ahead for her and Joy demonstrated her faith in God as she triumphed over every daily challenge.

Joy met every challenge, faced it head on, not necessarily willingly, but then quickly moved on to accepting the outcome. However profound her accomplishments, we were still a long way from living in the "normal" world. Here, in this hospital, she was a hero, an oddity, but a rarity and a hero as well. But we wondered what could or would she be when she was once again just a young girl going to school with her peers. How would they perceive her? Would she fit in? Would they accept her? Would she accept herself?

Joy and her mother

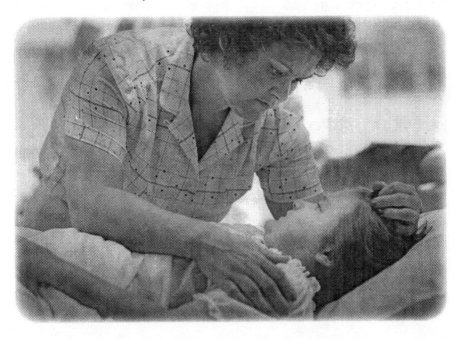

Photo appeared in July 1982 in the Philadelphia Inquirer

Chapter Nineteen

Another Amputation

Only a few days passed after the amputation of Joy's right leg when Dr. Watts once again called Ken and me into that "special" room to tell us that it was time to amputate the second leg. All the toes definitely had to come off and then the determination as to the length of the leg that could be left would be made while Joy was in the operating room. The orthopedic surgeons would amputate to good blood supply. As was the case in the first amputation, if the gangrenous area was not removed, the bacteria on the leg would enter her blood stream and compromise her life. This was just a basic rule of amputation. Although I knew this was going to happen by way of God's message to Joy — that she would walk and run and play on false legs — this was a breaking point for me. I just could not tell her, so I asked Ken to tell her. He did, and as I stood there with tears in my eyes, Joy looked me straight in the eye and said, "Mommy, don't worry. Everything will be all right." Joy's faith in God was so much a part of who she was now that even in these moments of being told that her left leg would be amputated tomorrow, she was attempting to comfort me, her grief-stricken mother.

That night before we went to sleep, Joy asked if I would listen to her nightly prayer which Tina and Joy said every night at home before going to sleep. I couldn't help thinking that Joy knew I could not pray right now because I was so distraught, so she intuitively asked if she could pray the pure and uncomplicated prayer she had memorized. As we held hands, bowed our heads and closed our eyes, Joy started talking to God by saying:

Now I lay me down to sleep
I pray the Lord my soul to keep
If I should die before I wake
I pray the Lord my soul to take

After Joy continued with her usual "God bless Mommy, Daddy, Tina," and proceeded until she named everyone in the family and then included a few of her new hospital friends, doctors and nurses, she closed as usual by saying...

I love you, Jesus.
And, thank You for taking care of my family and me.
Amen.

I was deeply touched by the realization that a child who was faced with such anguish and pain herself was able to bring peace to my soul through her simple little prayer.

The next day, her other leg was amputated just above her ankle. The heel pad from her foot that was amputated was reattached to the stump of her leg as a weight-bearing surface. This was her "long" leg. The other leg she nicknamed, "Shortie".

I am not exactly sure when, but at some point Joy was placed in traction. Each leg had a pin about 6 inches long through the leg and then out both sides. There was a bar above the bed that was attached to the ends of the bed to secure it. From the bar were two triangles that looked similar to the musical instruments that kindergarteners play. One was for each of Joy's legs. The pins in her leg were attached to these triangles. They held her legs in suspension to keep them from rubbing on the sheets and causing pain and to also help the amputations heal.

However, getting on and off the bedpan became more and more challenging. One day after surgery as we were waiting on the benches for Dr. Templeton to report how things went, we heard Joy screaming at the top of her lungs. Of course we thought she was either in excruciating pain or something even more devastating had just happened. When Dr. Templeton finally came out to talk to us, he calmed our fears by telling us that the nurses had put a catheter in Joy so that she did not have to use the bedpan. But since Joy had already shown her insistence on wearing her underpants, it followed logically that a catheter would not be a welcomed invasion. Sure enough, Joy pitched a fit until the recovery room nurses removed the catheter. Doctors and nurses let her win the battles they could.

Joy's pain was always a major issue. The pain she had to endure was unbearable. As I've written before, bone pain is excruciating pain. She had been given a PCA (patient controlled analgesia), which meant that she could administer a certain amount of pain medication to herself by pushing a button. Obviously, she could not have unlimited quantities, but knowing that she was in charge of providing some relief when she needed it really mattered. Along with the PCA, she often needed additional medication for excruciating pain. A great deal of my time was spent negotiating with the doctors to get pain medication for her. I appreciated that the doctors' concern was to prevent addiction, but addiction to me seemed to be a small matter at this point based on Joy's high degree of pain.

Her pain was measured on a scale of 1 to 10 — 10 being awful,

1, being no pain at all. She never had a 10 that I know of, which to me signified that although things were intolerable, she would not give in to her pain and say it was a 10. I became an expert about Joy's pain. I knew that if she said her pain was a 5 (which we calculated was actually 7) she could still tolerate it, but at 7 she could not (which was actually her 10). And having a 6 meant that 7 was not far away and something had to be done quickly before the pain got out of control. Pain needs to be managed well. If it gets out of control and you are chasing it, relieving the pain takes more medication than would have been necessary if the proper dose of pain medication had been administered at the 7 mark and the pain brought back under control. This was the vicious cycle Joy was in all the time. In 1982, pain medication was not liberally prescribed.

As I noted earlier, the deal I had made with myself was that I would care for Joy and her daily routine needs, and the nurses and the doctors then only needed to deal with her medication and medical needs. Since I was there around the clock, I kept to my deal, but when she needed pain medication, I would hunt down whoever was on duty and negotiate her pain medication until it got resolved. I was unrelenting! I felt I established a code that said, "I will not bother you unnecessarily, but when I come to you for help, it is of a serious and imminent nature. Please help now!"

Joy in her hospital room

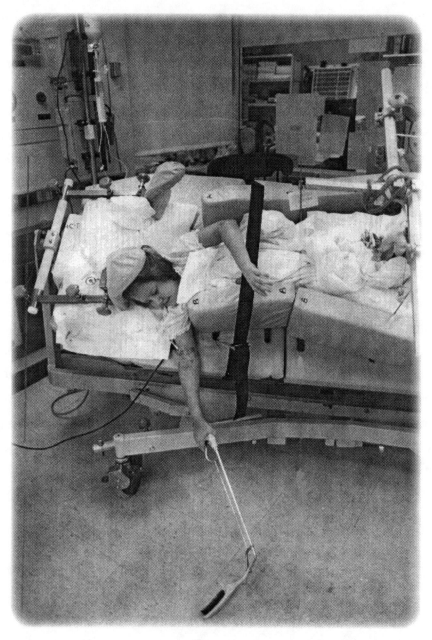

Photo appeared in July 1982 in the Philadelphia Inquirer

Chapter Twenty

A Hero at Seven

At this point we became aware of another component to our story. It was newsworthy! We were asked if Joy's story could be shared with others. "Little girl gets chicken pox, little girl almost dies, little girl lives instead. A story of profound courage." We had no idea that this was interesting. We were in a war against a disease and bacteria and had no idea the world wanted to know how the war was going. At the moment, we just couldn't see beyond the situation we were in until someone brought it to our attention that maybe others would want to know about this. Well, CHOP was an amazing hospital with many amazing people working here and this particular case was another one of those miracles to come out of this place. So we asked Joy if she would be willing to share her story, with limitations as to her physical exposure to protect her dignity.

Joy's story appeared on the Philadelphia area news channels and in Philadelphia newspapers as well as other regional and local papers at home. We were stunned by the response it brought from people we knew and then from many we never met. Apparently a little girl losing her legs due to a rare case of chicken pox was news. We were not reading about it. We were living the story and we were just doing what we had to do. Although the complication of the disease was such a rarity that it drew media attention, it was Joy's courage and positive attitude that people noticed, and the story tugged at their hearts. Because of her determination to fight and live, people willingly became involved. They wanted to be a part of the cheering section that encouraged her every day. They wanted to give her the recognition she deserved for having done something extraordinary.

The outpouring of sympathy, compassion and encouragement was unbelievable and very heartfelt. Cards and gifts were arriving for Joy in amazing quantities. Each time we moved from one hospital room to another, we had to pack up all of Joy's things. I remember filling over 12 large garbage bags with the gifts and cards she had received.

Various groups, such as one of the Philadelphia Mummer's Clubs, became aware of Joy through the news and came to play for her at the hospital. The Phillies baseball team signed a baseball and gave it to her. It was delightful to see the response to her struggle. So many celebrities and strangers shared with her a world she had never known before, a world filled with love for a little girl who was in the hospital and was suffering.

These gifts of love gave Joy an immediate sense of self-worth; although their concern and support could not be measured in material things, the prayers, cards and gifts certainly made a little girl and her family very happy. It was wonderful to know that all these people realized the magnitude of Joy's achievement as she beat the odds, she won over death, endured continuous surgeries and severe pain and overcame her own disfigurement. At seven years of age, Joy was a hero.

Meanwhile, a fundraising committee comprised of our family and friends, and representatives from the public relations department of our local hospital was formed to plan fundraisers to help offset our enormous hospital and medical bills. How sincerely touched we were that others realized our debt was mounting and began doing something about it.

Everyone helped. Even the medical staff of the hospital organized a car wash as a fundraiser and many of the doctors and the hospital staff washed the cars themselves. East Coast Salon Services sponsored another fundraiser. As an educational tool for hairstylists, a major distributor of beauty supplies will sponsor "hair shows" to provide information and education on products, styles and new techniques. This information is needed to meet the demands of an ever-changing fashion and beauty market. Since this distributor was one of the largest on the east coast, thousands and thousands of their customers, my peers, were invited to attend a benefit for Joy called, "Hair Style Marathon" while the Liberty Belles, cheerleaders for the Philadelphia Eagles football team, also gave a fashion show.

Since I was usually the one helping others, being on the receiving end was a new experience for me. I was ashamed of our financial situation and that we did not have insurance, but I had to put my pride aside and accept this generosity. I learned something invaluable: everyone needs help at one time or another in life and there are many kind and generous people who are willing to help. I was humbled. I never imagined myself being in this position, but here I was and I was so grateful for the assistance. Family, friends, clients and even strangers saw our need and went into action to do something about it.

In the end, because of the catastrophic level of Joy's medical problems and cost, the federal government agreed to pay the hospital a per diem and the hospital administrators agreed to accept it as payment in full! The doctors wrote off most of Joy's bill as well. When it was all said and done, because of the generosity and compassion of so many people, we owed very little to the hospital and the doctors. What an amazing blessing! The money that had been raised to help Joy went to help pay for her artificial legs, which at the time were $6,000 a pair. Because of her growth spurts and the changes taking place in her stumps, she had to have new legs about every 9 months for about 3 years. Our family, friends and community raised approximately $48,000, a huge fortune to us.

Back at the hospital where we were just beginning to adjust to Joy's new physical image, a support system of another kind was beginning to take form. It was as though God was moving His people to provide many of our needs even those we did not know existed. This group of friends and strangers had stories to tell Joy about their own losses and sufferings, their own physical and medical challenges and their own fears and victories. Quiet heroes, who may not have gotten any media recognition for overcoming their obstacles, contacted Joy to comfort her by sharing their struggles.

One by one supportive people came, as if an angel had gathered them for this purpose and sent them on a mission bearing a message that only they could deliver. Brave survivors of other ordeals came to share heartfelt and personal testimonies of their own struggles and challenges, yet rewards. One such person was my sister-in law, Mayra, who had breast cancer followed by a radical mastectomy. She told Joy that she was not the only person in our family who was an amputee. She showed Joy where her breast had been removed and explained why that needed to be done. She too was an amputee, she told Joy. I had never thought of her as an amputee. What an amazing and selfless thing for a woman to expose her body to a young child to let her know that she was not the only one who lost some part of her body through surgery. They had something in common, she told Joy. I know it comforted her.

Another good friend who had polio as a child came to see Joy to show her that she too had problems walking. Noreen explained to Joy that she got a disease as a young girl too. This disease caused her to have difficulty walking. She too had been sick for quite a while as a young child, but she went on to live a full life. She married a loving and caring man and now had four wonderful children. Joy confided in her that she wondered who would marry her. Noreen's loving response to Joy's question was that God surely had someone very special waiting for Joy.

And then another special person whom we did not know personally stopped in to see Joy. She, too, was quite remarkable. She was a young woman who had lost both of her legs in an automobile accident, yet walked into Joy's room with two of her children in tow. These were examples of real people who had survived and had overcome adversity and unexpected events in their lives and yet lived with love and hope. And Joy would too, they all told her.

Chapter Twenty-One

At Death's Door Once Again

The days passed, and every day and sometimes twice a day Joy would go to the OR for debriedement of the bacteria and every time Dr. Templeton would come out and talk to us, except this particular day in August. I sensed that something was wrong. We did not know it then, but the bacterial count was so high on her legs that it was eating away at the remaining muscle and tissue (Very little subcutaneous tissue was left and of course, no skin.) In the OR that day, the doctors had seriously contemplated the idea of amputating her legs at the groin. The bacteria was growing and spreading rapidly. Could such drastic amputation save her life? Her temperature had risen to 106 degrees and she had gone septic, which means the bacteria had entered her blood stream. She was moved back into ICU. Her last procedure was late that day and it was late in the evening when the chief surgical resident told Ken and me that they did not expect Joy to live through the night. In fact she had pneumonia as well, which prohibited them from taking her back into the OR for any more debriedement procedures. Now we understood what the bad news was.

As Joy's mother, I felt as though I was a part of a team trying to save her life. Sometimes we felt we could win and other times we felt defeated. This was a moment of defeat. And yet, I clearly recalled the promise God had made to Joy, so I was confused. Why would He tell her she would walk and run and play like other kids and then take her life?

As the realization hit that this could be it, I stood facing Dr. Charles Howe, the chief surgical resident, and pointed past him to Joy in her hospital bed. I said to him, "Do not attempt to save her life at any cost. Even though right now she is only 7, in that bed is somebody's grandmother. If there is not enough of her left for that, let her go. Do not do anything heroic to keep her alive." His response was, "I have never needed to make that decision. God will make it."

I left the room to tell my parents and family, who were out on the benches, what we had just been told. My mother immediately asked my brother to call their church's prayer chain to ask them to begin praying for Joy. I made her promise that they would instruct the people who would be praying to ask that God's will be done and not just to spare her life. If she were to be spared, let it be to function as a full human being, not just so I could go see her every day in some vegetative state.

It was a very long night. But, once again God made the decision. Without any explanation, Joy's condition began to turn around. Her temperature went down and she began to stabilize. As one of the doctors put it, "Something greater than us is in charge of this. I will tell you that we (the doctors, the nurses and the hospital staff) are not the ones in charge here, but Somebody is! We are merely just following after Him." We all knew what he meant — God was in charge and making the decisions. Anyone in this hospital had to know that something supernatural was going on.

Although attempts had been made to place skin grafts on Joy's legs, the grafts just sloughed off because the bacterial count was too high and the tissue was not healthy enough for them to adhere to the body. Even though the grafts did not "take", the sites where donor skin was removed were very painful. Thin layers of her skin were removed in patches from her breastbone down. Then the pieces of skin were put through a machine that would stretch them and "waffle" them so that they would cover more area. The donor sites of the grafts burn like a brush burn. Since so much of her body was donor sites for her legs and she was hanging in traction, she was extremely uncomfortable and in pain. And yet we all knew that this skin grafting was what had to be done to get Joy to the point where she could go home. Since this round of skin grafts did not take, another attempt could hopefully be made when the legs were healthier. But when would that happen? How could that happen?

Having pneumonia, Joy could not be anesthetized, so the new procedure for removal of the bacteria was to do it manually —scrub it away. Ouch! OUCH! She had no skin on her legs, so this was excruciating. A new level of pain had been reached! Reluctantly, every day and sometimes twice a day, the doctors would roll the bandage cart into the room for the bandage change. Each procedure was beyond painful for Joy and for everyone in the room who had to hear her screams of pain and anguish. Everyone dreaded it. Yet it was just another thing that had to be done. Before the team arrived for the bandage change, she would be given a bolus of 7.5 ml of morphine just in time to take effect before they would begin. This was in addition to the morphine drip that she was already receiving for pain control. The timing had to be accurate so that the pain medication would take effect. Then the process would start and the bandage team would scrub her legs, hopefully free of the bacteria. Obviously it was nerve racking for everyone. She seemed to be able to hear that bandage cart being wheeled down the hall from a mile away. Then her anxiety would begin.

It wasn't long before one of the child psychiatrists came to see us — on the benches. He told us how disturbing the bandage changes were for those who had to be in the room. Something had to be done. I asked him if he had ever been in the room when they were changing her bandages. "No," he said. He had actually never met her. I suggested that he attend one. He arrived for the bandage change in an attempt to understand how to control Joy's outbreak of screaming. I remained on the bench. The bandage change began as did the screaming and within a few minutes the child psychiatrist was out of the room and rushing past me on the bench. I yelled out to halt him. He looked back at me with a horrified look on his face, as he kept hurriedly retreating from this scene as though he was scared to death. However, he did glance back over his shoulder and gasp, "I cannot talk to you right now. I do not know how she can stand it."

Being the wonderful people that they were, the doctors and the nurses devised a plan that would help ease Joy's anxiety. Since they were "hurting" her, she should be able to retaliate in some way. So they gave Joy a water gun to use to squirt them when they hurt her. Next, they began singing the song " 99 Bottles of Beer On The Wall" so that she had an idea as to what bottle of beer was still on the wall when they would be finished. This helped. She needed to know how long this pain was going to last.

Since she had pneumonia from being in bed so long, she was placed in a special bed that rotated 45 degrees. It was in constant motion. Even the solutions to the problems created more exhausting obstacles to jump over and new obstacles were arriving all the time. Taking care of her toilet needs and feeding her while the bed was rotating was difficult. Along with this, her legs that were still in traction would sway with every move of the bed. However, the rotating bed did help, and along with the right antibiotics, the pneumonia was cleared.

Interestingly, Ken and I each focused on entirely different issues relating to Joy's care. The same areas of strength that helped us with our businesses were the areas we drew on for Joy's care. Ken focused on the day-to-day details while I was the concept person. I didn't see what he saw and he didn't see what I saw. He would examine how the bed was positioned and how the traction was angled and whether it was comfortable for her and if not, what could be changed. He would agonize over her day-to-day necessities while I would be trying to process and plan how she would live the rest of her life in this new body of hers. Each of us had a job to do and we did it to our best ability. We wanted to believe we were a necessary part of her recovery.

Another amazing thing was about to happen. Dr. Templeton had contacted a physician friend of his who had begun harvesting amnion, the lining of the placenta, to help burn victims. Joy's condition made her similar to a child who had been severely burned with the loss of her skin and tissue. Since skin is the natural biological covering to keep bacteria out of the body and since it is the only organ that cannot be transplanted from one person to another (at least not in 1982), and since Joy's own skin grafts could not take hold because of the amount of bacteria growing on her body, some biological covering had to be found. Dr Templeton's friend discovered that amnion could be separated from the placenta (harvested) after the birth of a baby and placed on the wound or body of someone needing skin as the new biological barrier to bacteria. Dr. Templeton had a team of residents go out to the area hospitals and "harvest" the placentas. This task was not easy. To harvest amnion required separating this egg-white type film from the inner lining of the placenta just after the birth of a healthy baby.

Each lining was about a 4x4 piece of filmy tissue. Many pieces were needed for Joy to have coverage on her limbs and hopefully stop the bacterial growth.

The team of residents brought the amnion back to CHOP and placed it on Joy's legs. In a matter of 24 hours the bacterial count on her legs went from millions per square inch to zero. It was beyond incredible! These amnion-dressing changes quickly became routine and so did the harvesting. We were thrilled that Dr. John Templeton and his team of doctors were willing to undertake such an unprecedented method to save her life and limbs. The amnion provided such a good barrier from the bacteria that her own tissue became healthy and would then accept skin grafts. She was again grafted using donor sites from her own body and this time the grafts took. She now had the most bizarre looking "stumps", but they were on their way to healing and hopefully someday could be fitted for prostheses. The assumption was that she would need years of physical therapy before she could possibly consider walking. She had lost so much of her muscle, skin and tissue that the doctors would not even speculate that she would ever walk again.

It was still summertime and Joy was once again moved out of ICU into a room on the patients' floor. These improvements were small steps, but they were nevertheless steps that meant she was doing better. She spent most of the four and a half months she was in the hospital in ICU. After she got settled in her new room, her next step towards recovery was to go to physical therapy for whirlpool baths to keep the legs clean and to help promote good circulation. Whirlpool baths sound like a wonderful idea for someone relaxing at a spa. However, for someone with no skin on her legs (the grafts had not grown shut yet) being placed in a tub of swirling water HURTS! Imagine how painful putting a finger with a small cut on it in water feels. Now imagine no skin on your legs and submersing legs without skin on them in swirling water.

The pain was unimaginable. Pain was always considered and somewhat managed, but the degree of pain that Joy experienced would be so unbearable that the amount of medication that she could be given for her body size could in no way be enough to eliminate the pain. She just had to endure it. I clearly remember the first time Dr. Templeton told me she was going to the whirlpool. She had just come out of recovery from surgery. Dr. Templeton knew more clearly than I her medical condition and that the bacteria had to be removed from her legs. She had to have whirlpool baths to clean the surface of her legs and to remove as much bacteria as possible.

Intellectually I knew he was right, but I lost it! It was one of the times when I thought I could not bear her suffering one more thing. I responded to this idea of the whirlpool like Joy's mother rather than a member of her medical support team. My eyes welled up with tears and my lower lip started to tremble. Since I had been accepted as a member of Joy's medical support team, my emotion was not appreciated. I remember Dr. Templeton, a man of few words, looking me directly in the eye and saying more or less, "If you are going to act like that (emotionally or out of control), you may not come along."

Well, I had been given the ultimatum. Generally I was permitted access to almost every area of the hospital that was appropriate for me to be in and I didn't want that to change. I knew I had to just pull myself up by the bootstraps and march forward. There was no time for me to regain their respect if I were to fall apart. So I took some deep breaths and somehow regained my composure in time to go with them to the whirlpool to hold her hand and listen to her screams until the treatments were over. Painful but essential, whirlpool baths were another addition to her care that went on every day. How could I go home knowing what she would then face alone? My feeling was, if she could handle it, so would I.

Along with all of these other things going on, Joy also lost most of her hair. The few strands left on each side of her head were pulled up into very sparse pigtails. When her hair did finally start to grow back, it was gray! It was presumed to be a result of "shock". All of her daily events were quite traumatizing for sure, but I wasn't completely convinced that shock was the reason for her hair discoloration.

Since I was in the beauty industry and knew about Redken's laboratory in California specializing in the chemistry of hair, I called the lab from the pay phone in the hall and spoke to one of the scientists, briefly explaining Joy's health and medical problems and that her hair was presently coming in gray. I further explained that Joy had not eaten regular food for months because of the daily surgeries and that she was being intravenously fed hyperalimentation, a complete liquid nutritional food supplement. The scientist in California responded with a suggestion for the hyperalimentation formulation to include a slightly different combination of amino acids which they knew to determine color pigmentation of hair. The hospital lab at CHOP responded to the suggestion and slightly altered the hyperalimentation formula. Joy's hair began to grow back in its original color, blonde. Of all the traumatic things that happened to Joy throughout this whole experience, she still vividly recalls how devastated she was over losing her hair and its color.

Chapter Twenty-Two

A Day Pass

Thank you, God! For the most part, by September, the daily crises seemed to be under control. I stayed in the hospital with Joy, and Ken returned home to be with Tina who had just begun sixth grade. We had started to renovate our bedroom and part of our family room when the crisis with Joy happened. Ken went home to try to put our house back together. We hoped that our lives would be put back in some normal order soon and we could return home.

Until now, all of our energies had been spent helping Joy survive. The thought of going home was just beginning to creep into our minds. It was not a reality to us until someone told us about a day pass. A day pass could be given to a patient (a child, since we were in Children's Hospital) to leave the hospital for a specific number of hours and then return. Joy and I decided that we would inquire about this. Could we really get out of the hospital and go home? We floated the idea with the docs and they said that we could go home on a day pass...after the whirlpool treatment. Getting through the pain of the whirlpool that day had new meaning. We were going home! With jubilation in my voice, I called Ken and Tina, to gleefully inform them that Joy and I would be coming home! Joy got a day pass! We couldn't believe it! After more than four months in the hospital, we were going home!

Since we had no idea that this could happen, we had no clothes other than hospital gowns for Joy to wear. Joy entered the hospital in May, a "normal" six- year-old with two legs and a full head of hair. She was leaving the hospital having turned seven while in the hospital (June 2) minus feet, minus parts of both of her legs which were fully bandaged, missing most of the skin and subcutaneous tissue on both legs, having donor sites which left permanent scars on her upper body, having a very full face from the steroids making her barely resemble herself, and having only a few strands of hair. We had not actually realized until this moment that she was rather bizarre looking according to "normal" standards. But she was ALIVE!

We made arrangements to borrow a wheelchair from the hospital for our time home since we obviously did not need one before we came to the hospital. In fact, this was the first realization that many things had changed for us. We now had a disabled child. We needed to adapt our minds, our home and our future to accommodate our new situation. Joy had become a celebrity at CHOP and she deserved to be elevated to that. However, what would the world outside the hospital think of her? And as the years passed and she was no longer some cute little girl who made headlines because of her bravery, could her peers still embrace her as a whole person? We would soon discover the answers to these questions.

But today, we just wanted to go home. I lifted Joy into the car and placed the wheel chair in the back of my station wagon. The car had been parked in the garage under the hospital for over four months. God forgive me, but I realized that if I told the parking garage that I lost my parking ticket, I would only pay for one full day of parking in the garage instead of four months. Having very little money on me, that is exactly what I did and we were on our way.

What struck me as we drove up out of the underground garage into the daylight was the small patch of grass that was in my view directly across the street. Since we were in center city, there was very little grass, but I remember thinking how green it was. Had the grass actually gotten greener while Joy was in the hospital? Of course not! I just seemed to see it and appreciate it for the first time in my life. I stuck my head out the window hoping to get a whiff of it. How odd that seems now, but back then I was re-entering a life I had left behind and I was seeing things and appreciating them as I had never done before. Life would never look the same to me.

Although I did not know how we would make it financially or how we would actually be able to meet the challenges that were before us, I knew with great assurance that the God who was with us through these last four months was in the car with us now too. Miracles had taken place and more miracles were needed to make this all work out. Right at this moment it was a miracle that we were leaving the hospital. Joy did not die. Instead, she was going home.

Home was a 30-minute ride. We laughed and talked about what the first thing was that she wanted to do. After all, this was her big day. She told me she wanted to see her best friend, Mindy Gensler. In fact, she wanted to stop and pick her up to take her to our house to play. Play. Although every attempt was made by the hospital to provide a play time, play therapist and a playroom for Joy to experience being a child in the midst of having to be stronger than most adults, there was still nothing like picking up her best friend and playing together the way they used to. Could they? I decided to let them decide that.

We pulled into Mindy's driveway, unannounced, of course. Leaving Joy in the car, I went to the door and knocked. An absolutely wonderful woman, Phyllis, Mindy's mother, answered the door. She was as surprised to see us as we were to be there. Although she and Mindy had visited us in the hospital and were very aware of our situation, they did not expect us to be home yet. I told Phyllis of Joy's interest in having Mindy come home with us and asked if it would be all right. Mindy had already slipped out between us and made a beeline for the car where Joy was anxiously waiting to see her best friend. In that instant it occurred to me that Joy looked more like an alien than the friend Mindy remembered. I would have understood the reluctance of this seven year old to accompany her friend home. Remember, Joy didn't even have regular clothes on, which could have helped the situation. She was still in hospital gowns, one open in the back and one open in the front acting as a bathrobe to cover all exposed areas.

The two girls started to chat and giggle like old times. I still am not clear if Mindy said yes to coming over willingly or if she just found herself ushered into the car by her very wise and loving mother, but the two friends were reunited. The conversation between the two was what were they going to play when they got to our house. Mindy asked a few questions as to how Joy would get around since she had no feet now. She was interested in the fact that Joy had a new means of transportation, a wheel chair. Noting this, Joy suggested that they take turns pushing each other in the wheel chair. Immediately after making this suggestion Joy caught herself and said, "Mindy, I can't push you in the wheel chair. I have no feet. You can push me if you like and then we'll go inside and play." I was amazed at how quickly they both adapted to the new situation.

We arrived at the house and were greeted by Ken and Tina. All of us were beside ourselves with glee, but a bit apprehensive as well. How would Joy get around? Was our home accessible for her and the wheel chair? We were in uncharted waters now. But on this special day we just wanted to enjoy being home. We sat in our family room watching TV, talking and nibbling treats from our own kitchen while Tina, Joy and Mindy sat on the floor and played with Joy's Barbie dolls.

We returned to the hospital that night with a renewed sense of hope. Although our time at home was limited to a few hours, it was the beginning of the realization that we would return permanently. We would be a family again. And we could begin dreaming once more about the future.

Joy and Mindy — 1998

Chapter Twenty-Three

Our First Family Outing

The movie ET came out in 1982 and, like most other children, Joy wanted to see it. However, she complained loudly about her donor sites. These very painful areas on her body, where skin had been removed for grafting, constantly irritated Joy. They felt like really bad scrapes from falling off a bike, but these donor sites involved her entire body.

As was explained previously, the split thickness skin, as it was termed, was not a full thickness of skin, but a thin section of skin which was sliced from the body, then meshed to increase the size of it by punching holes in it to make it larger and more pliable to cover more area. This donated skin becomes a graft of skin. Although these grafts of donated skin "took," the skin itself was very thin and delicate. Over the years this thin grafted skin would be a major problem for Joy. Being an amputee with good skin could mean good circulation and a good stump. Joy had thin tight skin on her stumps, poor circulation and many, many breakdowns, because the skin was not thick enough or pliable enough for the friction that would occur from wearing the prostheses.

Despite her discomfort and annoying pain, Joy wanted to go to the movies. Although Ken and I appeared as though we had things under control, inside we were jittery. We had never maneuvered a person in a wheel chair before and did not always know what obstacles would get in our way. As a family, we decided to go to the movies in the afternoon. I explained to Joy that being out in public meant that a certain behavior was expected from her. If she were in too much pain or discomfort, we would stay home. But if she wanted to go, she could not complain about her donor sites during the movie. Other people had to be considered. She promised that she could contain herself and off we went. We did not realize that in our new situation, with a child in a wheel chair, more time would be required to get out of the car and to our destination. As a result, we were a few minutes late to the movie and the previews had started. The lights were off and the theatre was in total darkness. Ken agreed to push Joy, and we started down the aisle to a place in the theatre where we could all sit yet still leave the wheel chair in the aisle, hoping that no one would stumble on it. We were as quiet as we possibly could be, but one thing we soon learned is that when someone is in a wheel chair, people gawk and stare. In Joy's present condition, we got a lot of stares. How often does one see a little hairless girl with no legs? Some things we just couldn't hide. So, we got plenty of stares even in the darkened movie theatre. It seemed that we made a grand entrance everywhere we went — unintentionally.

Ken pushed Joy cautiously down the aisle, followed very closely behind by Tina and myself. We were already developing a false sense of security since we had successfully accomplished getting to the movie theatre and down the aisle and now were anxious to soon be in our seats. Being new at all of this, we were often glad when we accomplished what was for others a simple little family outing. Yet, for us, each family outing was a major undertaking and constant learning experience.

Well, before I knew it there was a big collision and pile-up of people in the aisle. In the dark, we could not see another wheel chair with a person in it in the aisle. Our parade of people with Joy and wheel chair in the lead almost toppled over the wheel chair and person in front of us in the aisle hidden by the darkness. As Tina and I struggled to keep our balance and not land on top of each other in a heap, I thought," So much for quiet social conduct in public." No one was hurt, and we chuckled about this many times later. Nevertheless, the movie was exactly what we needed, filled with love and wonder and seemingly impossible accomplishments. As we watched ET sitting on the handlebars of the bike being "driven" by Elliott and flying high into the sky, I too felt as though my feet did not touch the ground all the time from the sheer excitement of our own impossible accomplishments. However, for Joy, there was only reality. Her feet never touched the ground.

As the days in the hospital finally came to an end around September 26, we said goodbye to our many friends and a surreal world where we were safe medically and emotionally. Now we would begin a life of uncertainty that our hearts longed for. Home at last. At home we continued the bandage changes with the amnion. I got pretty good at separating the egg white type substance and placing it on her legs. We made trips to Allentown, Pennsylvania, to pick up more amnion, this life saving substance. We were spending over $200 a week on bandages. The stress did not go away. It just changed. It was very important to remember that this is what we wanted. We wanted to be together as a family and every sacrifice we made for our children would be a willing sacrifice. No matter what material things we lost or what economic situation we would later find ourselves suffering through, we considered all of these sacrifices worth it.

I can appreciate how difficult it is to go from one set of devastating circumstances to another. I guess respite is necessary. I honor that; I just never had the privilege of experiencing it. What we had overcome was exhilarating, but ahead was a battle for a lifetime. I could not pause to discern how tired I was or how hard it had been. The next battlefront was already here and we were behind in the war. The challenge of daily living, surviving financially, working through it, resurrecting the business, paying enormous debt, buying necessary medical supplies and even paying to park to go to the continuous doctors' visits for Joy were enough of a burden to send us into a permanent tailspin. What kept me going was the promise God made to Joy that she would walk and run and play like other kids on false legs.

We had a date with destiny. Since God had kept her alive, I felt that no matter what would lie ahead, no matter what the impossible challenges, she could live out her life victoriously because of His promises to her.

Chapter Twenty-Four

Joy Walks!

In early October, just weeks after Joy was released from the hospital, but before I went back to work, a new client, John, arrived at Creative Image Salon, my salon in Moorestown. Ann, the stylist cutting John's hair, struck up a conversation with him and discovered he was a doctor. The conversation turned to Children's Hospital of Philadelphia, where he had recently finished a residency in anesthesiology. Hearing this, Ann began to talk about Joy and asked John if he knew of her. "Of course I do," he stated solemnly, "But I left CHOP at a time when she was critically ill because my rotation was over. How sad it was for her to die," he sighed. Ann promptly and happily responded, "Die? Oh, no, she didn't die. She's very much alive!" With that John stood up, turned around to face Ann in utter shock and surprise. Totally amazed that Joy had survived, he begged for more details. "How is she doing now?" he petitioned. "Is she home from the hospital? Could I possibly see her?" Joy's condition was so critical during his rotation that her death seemed a certainty.

When Ann called Ken and me about this conversation, we immediately arranged a time to meet John in the parking lot next to the salon. Through the large window in front of the salon, John could see us pull up in our car. Eagerly he came out of the salon and approached our car. Ken got out to greet him. I was sitting in the passenger's seat holding Joy on my lap. John peered into the car window to see Joy. He said hello to her and immediately lowered his eyes to look intently at her legs. I knew he was looking to see if the orthopedic surgeons had amputated her legs at the groin, which was the only recourse he knew of since she had survived. John was astonished to see that the proposed amputation of Joy's legs to the groin had not been done, and her stumps were still below her knees. Clearly he was delighted and impressed that such a miracle had happened.

Although Ken and I were exuberant that Joy's condition was better than had been expected and that she was doing remarkably well so soon after being discharged from the hospital, Ken and I knew we had other obstacles to leap over. We had to begin the process of putting our lives back together and that meant going back to work. Ken and I talked about which one of us should return to the businesses and which one of us would stay home with Joy.

We decided that I should go back to work at this point. Tina was in school all day and Joy only required daily routine childcare, which Ken was capable of handling. The daily bandage changes could be done when I came home from work. It was difficult to imagine us living a normal life again. What was "normal" going to be for us now? We didn't know, but we had to try and figure it out.

Only two weeks had passed since I had returned to work at the salon when Joy called to tell me something very exciting had just happened. She informed me that she had walked from our family room to the phone, a distance of about 12 feet. What? How could that be possible? The only way I had seen her get around the house was to crawl or to wheel herself in the wheel chair wherever it could fit in our home. Joy explained that her father had gone to our garage and made her a set of crutches. Then, he changed her stump protectors around, putting the short one on the long leg and the long one on the short leg, making the two legs an equal distance from the floor. The stump protectors were semi-round bottomed clear plastic casts designed for her to wear so that if she accidentally banged her legs on something around the house, she would not compromise the grafts or the tender stumps that had not totally healed.

So with the aid of her homemade crutches and the plastic stump protectors that now made her legs appear the same length, she was upright and moving. That was miraculous!

Ken's most admirable attribute was his adventurous attitude towards trying something new. A few years before this happened to Joy, we took the girls skiing. Although they were quite young, Ken encouraged them to try skiing. "Don't be afraid to try something difficult and new," he encouraged the girls. And with his encouragement, they succeeded in the sport. He brought adventure into their lives. Therefore, it was within his character to get Joy moving, trying something new and challenging.

Almost exactly two weeks later, Joy once again called me at work to tell me she had just walked from the family room to the phone in the kitchen. "Honey," I replied gently, "That's great, but I already know you have been doing that with your stump protectors and your crutches." " NO, Mommy," she responded, "this time I did it without my crutches!" Was she actually walking on those round-bottomed stump protectors? Could she actually balance herself on those devastated legs? Did she actually have the body strength to do it? YES! How could this be? What was she standing on? What was holding her up? After all, the doctors said it could take years of physical therapy. They even implied that she might never have adequate muscle and strength in her limbs to ever walk. Then I remembered both God's promise to her and the words of a song I used to sing in church,

Standing on the promises I cannot fall
Listening every moment to the Spirit's call
Resting in my Savior as my all in all
Standing on the promises of God.

Joy was indeed standing on God's promises to her and they were holding her up and moving her forward. Praise God!

We quickly called Dr. Watts, her orthopedist, and made an appointment for him to see what we had witnessed. We did not tell him why we were coming.

Joy was everyone's sweetheart at CHOP, so it was not unusual to have a large group of people just stop by to say hello when she was in the hospital for any reason. Such was the case today. Orthopedic examining rooms were rather long and narrow so that the therapist or doctor could watch the patient walk to improve the patient's ambulation if at all possible. Dr. Watts and his team entered the room for what they assumed was a problem that needed resolution. After all, this particular patient was Joy, who was filled with unresolved issues. We requested the doctors and those who came to say hello to Joy to remain in the doorway to the examining room. At the opposite end of the room was Joy, sitting down. Heads were bobbing all over the place at the doorway as people gathered to peer over the crowd to wave and smile at Joy.

When the crowd settled down and we had everyone's attention, Ken told Joy, "Okay, go ahead." With that, and with all eyes on Joy, she got up from the chair and step by step walked to the stunned, then wildly applauding, group gathered at the other end of the room. To say there was not a dry eye in the place would understate the emotions of all witnesses to this walking miracle.

Dr. Watts responded by saying, "Take her to the prosthetic

department and get her measured for a set of legs." Over the bandages and skin grafts, Joy was cast for a set of prostheses. On November 19, 1982, we went to the hospital to pick up her new legs, fully expecting to bring them home so that she could practice using them to help her walk. However, Joy had something else in mind. She put them on and instantly began walking around the hospital. Her first stop was to the OR to see Dr. John Templeton.

We were all amazed to see how quickly she adapted to walking on these artificial legs. For Joy to walk so soon would have been viewed as unbelievable, amazing or even impossible had we not already crossed over those waters into "Anything's possible with Joy". No one set boundaries for her. This was very important. "Let her decide what she can or cannot do," was the unspoken rule, and she was doing just that. Her legs were clearly missing from her body, but her desire to walk and get on with her life was clearly not missing. Joy made the rules that worked for her and no one tried to stop her or even redirect her, not even caution her. She was moving full speed ahead and we were all in awe of her. At seven years of age she was teaching us how to overcome the impossible, how to accept oneself in new circumstances, and how to deal with new disabilities. There was life for her to live and she was running towards it.

Joy wanted to walk as much as she possibly could. How much was that? Who knew? I often took her to work with me so that she could walk down the sidewalk outside the salon. This day we decided to walk the half block to the toy store. Once we were walking together, I realized that Joy kept looking down at her feet. Since I did not possess a full knowledge of how prostheses actually work, I was nervous about her being so bent over because I thought she might topple right to the ground. I was on a learning curve as well.

However, even after voicing my concern to her, she kept staring at her feet as we walked along.

Finally, after tthinking she had studied her feet long enough, I asked her why she was staring at her feet. Without hesitation she replied, "Mommy, I have to look at my feet so that when someone steps on them, I will know when to say, 'Ouch!'" Sounded reasonable to me.

Joy and her first new legs

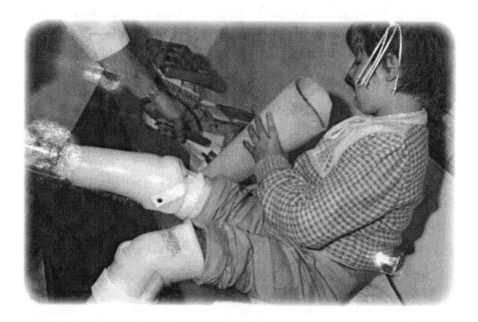

Joy and new legs

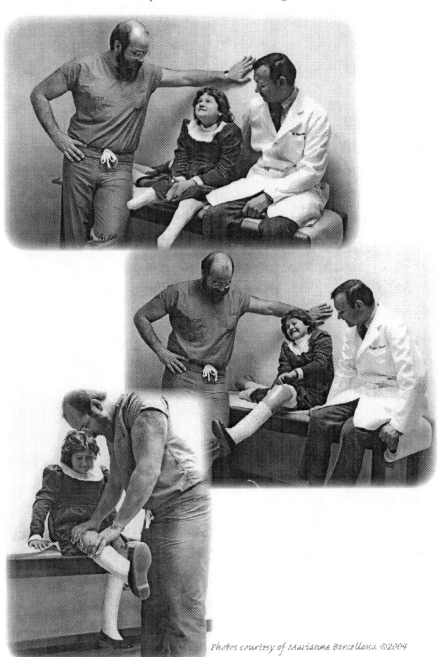

Photos courtesy of Marianne Barcellona ©2004

Chapter Twenty-Five

Tina: Faithful Daughter & Fantastic Sister

In January, Joy returned to school. She had missed from May 2 until the end of school in her kindergarten year and the first half of first grade. It was time to go back. Every step of re-entering a normal life was so extremely important to all of us.

Tina was very anxious about Joy's return to school. She was aware of her sister's new appearance and was concerned for her. Because Joy had no legs, Tina was worried about how she would be treated since she was different from other first graders. Tina observed the glances and stares of the kids as they met Joy with approval or rejection. When Joy was fully clothed, she almost resembled a person without a disability, but with her hair still missing and her face very puffy from the steroids, she still looked different from the other students. Although Joy's story had been told on major news channels and in local and regional papers and almost everyone locally knew it, Tina wondered if the kids really understood and would accept her sister.

Tina's life changed after the birthday party we had for Joy shortly after Joy returned home. Even though Joy's birthday was June 2, we celebrated the special day in October because Joy had been in the hospital in June. The party was a real success. A regional TV station caught wind of it and arrived at our house to film the party for the evening news. All the little girls attending the birthday party were excited to be on TV. Joy had not gotten her legs yet, so she was "standing" on her knees while her friends, of course, were standing on their feet. I am sure although the party was fun, the TV coverage and the anticipation of the guests appearing on the evening news was even more exciting.

However, when the cameras left and it was time to "just be girls", one little girl began sobbing and wanted to go home. When I tried to comfort her and find out what had happened, she said that she was afraid of Joy. "Joy looks weird. She's scary looking," the little girl said. Tina was close by and heard this. Ken and I could sympathize with the little girl and called her mother to pick her up.

However, Tina took on a role that she never gave up from that point on, and that was to defend Joy and to protect her from the glares and insults of people who did not understand. I believe it was at this moment that Tina, this gentle sensitive young girl, became Joy's protective watchdog, capable of biting and snarling when necessary to tell others to keep back or adjust their attitude. Sadly, her youth and innocence was gone too. Tina's personality was being defined and developed through her experience with Joy.

Tina was our first-born. She only weighed 4 lbs. 14 oz at birth. She had dark blonde hair and the most beautiful hazel-green eyes I had ever seen. They were light green hazel eyes with a dark outer rim. We brought her home from the hospital to my parents' home where we lived for about a year while our house was being built. My father was so excited to have her live with them. In fact, it reminded me of how excited he was when my sister was born. My dad loved babies. I remember hearing about the day he went to a customer's home to do some work. The customer had a baby who had fallen asleep under his crib. My dad got down on his hands and knees to peek under the crib to see the baby. We could count on a certain twinkle being present in his eyes whenever there was a baby or young child around. Tina became his next permanent twinkle.

Moving day finally came. Our house was finished and it was time to leave my parents' home to go to our new home. My father would not help us move, which was out of character for him. He had helped us with everything before. Instead he sat on the side of his bed with his head bent down, not moving or saying anything. Finally I went up to him to tell him that everything was packed and we were ready to leave. He did not raise his head to say good-bye. He merely said, "You can leave if you want. But can't you leave her here?" He, of course, meant Tina. He was heartbroken that she was leaving even though we were only moving 10 miles down the road. Obviously, we came to see them often. Dad would always come out to greet us, but his real interest was in plucking Tina from the car and getting her back into his arms. I can still see my dad walking from the car into their house holding Tina's little hand as she toddled beside him. Both were very happy. Each time she came to visit, the twinkle came back into his eyes.

Tina was a very pleasant child and very cute. She was far from demanding and clearly did not have a demonstrative personality. She did not have to have her own way either. As she became more developed, we enrolled her in gymnastics where she excelled. At the age of seven, she was small enough in stature and weight to be able to perform extremely well. I was always amazed watching her do back flips across the living room floor. Her instructor saw something in her worth developing and pushed her to train and to compete. However, the rigorous training required for serious competition completely changed the way Tina felt about the sport. She cried all the way to the gym, while she was there, and on the way home. It was time to rethink why she was doing this. She wanted to quit because she did not possess an aggressive or competitive spirit.

Tina was gentle and non-aggressive as a child. However, when this crisis happened to Joy and afterwards, Tina became a warrior. She reminded me of my mother, who was gentle, but the experiences in her own life forced her outside her area of comfort onto the battlefield. My mother did what she had to do, not what was comfortable for her. Tina heroically did the same thing. Her defense of Joy became her new focus and now defined her personality. About a year after Joy came home from the hospital, Ken returned to his habit of excessive drinking, which kept him out late several nights a week. Unknown to me, Tina assumed the role of mother to Joy as I assumed the role of father and provider to our family. These new roles were not decided consciously, but out of necessity.

Tina's choices of friends were often based on the friend's ability to understand the real world, the world of pain and suffering. Tina had no patience with people who complained about trifling things. Only those who knew and understood the Joy story and could cope with it and be compassionate toward it could be considered in Tina's circle of friends. In fact, Liz Besnoff, who remains Tina's best friend to this day, was one such individual. Tina could turn to Liz for support and compassion for herself and Joy during these many, many crises.

Tina's friends didn't always consist of her peers. She sought the friendship and undying devotion of Liz's mother, Jenny, and embraced Joanne Fowler, her cousin, as her surrogate mother. Tina deserved to have people in her life who could sooth her pain in a gentle and loving manner. Most moments in Tina's life were of a serious nature. She wisely chose these women, Liz, Jenny and Joanne, to help her bear the burdens she so willingly endured for her family. These women supported Tina by showering her with the gentleness of their touch, the softness of their voices and the kindness of their willing hearts to console her. Tina would turn to them time and again to renew her spirit and calm her soul, and their love, wisdom and friendship were always a tremendous comfort to her. I pray that God will bless them abundantly for the love and compassion they have shown my daughter.

I sincerely regret how much Tina and her childhood were eclipsed by Joy's medical problems. But I have seen a woman grown out of a child and I am in awe of her strength and willingness to sacrifice for others. Tina could have chosen to take a different road and resent the attention given to Joy, abandon our struggle, and live her own life. She certainly deserved that as everyone does. But within her was God's strength and enormous love for her family. May we always be worthy of her tremendous sacrifice.

Joy and Tina in 1982 and 2001

Top photo courtesy
of Marianne Barcellona © 2004

Chapter Twenty-six

Back to School

Back at the school, the child study team was evaluating Joy so that they could accommodate her special needs. They concluded in their report that Joy was indeed physically challenged. Obviously. Yet there was something else on the report. It stated that she was also psychologically impaired. "Where did that come from?" I asked. Well, nothing formally indicated that, I was told, but wouldn't you expect that to be the case? One evaluator added, "Who could go through what she went through and not be psychologically impaired?"

"I don't know about someone else and how they would respond to the situation, but I know about Joy," I replied. I informed them that I could provide as much data as they needed to prove that she was not psychologically impaired. I told them of the doctor in the hospital who had been there for many years and had dealt with patients who had become disfigured. His comment to me personally was, "I have never before seen anyone become so disfigured and not go psychotic." It was then they agreed to take the statement out of Joy's evaluation.

In preparing for Joy's return to school, I understood that the child study team was attempting to provide the very best learning environment for Joy. But her orthopedic challenges needed to be addressed first and then, secondly, any absences from school or gaps in her education that her condition might create.

Joy was doing well and was very happy to be back. She still

had many medical demands, doctors' appointments, visits to the prothetist for adjustments, and trips to the hospital, so she missed a great deal of school. When she went for these various appointments I, of course, went with her so my work schedule and workday was never guaranteed to take place the way it needed to. If Joy could not go to school because of her condition, which still needed my attention, I stayed home with her.

If we went for an appointment somewhere, there was no telling when we would arrive home. Would we be gone two hours or six hours? Tina could not rely on us being home at any specific time, and then she would begin to worry about us. Were they keeping Joy in the hospital? Would we be coming home tonight? How long would we be staying? Our new situation was the beginning of a different life. It was a life completely void of routine. None of us knew that tomorrow we could get up, shower, eat breakfast, get ready for work and school and actually go. Joy's medical needs were demanding and often sudden. Although we became terrific survivors, we were lousy at living in the "normal routine" world, but we never gave up trying. I also had to earn a living, somehow. I knew that my heavenly Father was very wealthy and He did not bring us this far for us to fall on our heads now. He would provide.

Although things were out of the ordinary, there was some balance. Exciting things happened too. As our pendulum of life was swinging far to the left into the tragedy, pain and suffering area, it was also swinging up to the right every bit as high into the area of "thrilled to be alive".

Joy at home

Photos at top appeared in the
Philadelphia Inquirer, Dec. 1982.
Bottom photo courtesy of
Marianne Barcellona ©2004

Chapter Twenty-Seven

Going Skiing

Skiing? Joy is going skiing? Is that possible? Joy had her legs amputated in June 1982, got home from the hospital in September, got her prostheses in November and now in March she was going skiing? The 52 Association from New York in conjunction with the 7-Eleven, Southland Corporation, contacted Joy and offered her a free skiing trip. The 52 Association was an advocacy group for amputees aimed at encouraging them to participate in sports and to gain confidence through sports activities even after losing a limb. At the time, most of their participants were Vietnam Veterans who became amputees in the war. However, other amputees were welcomed. The organization sponsored three-day ski programs at Jack Frost Mountain in White Haven, Pennsylvania. Since we had skied as a family before Joy became an amputee, we were interested to discover whether or not it would be possible for us to enjoy the sport again as a family.

We also knew that Joy skiing so soon after her amputations, surgeries and skin grafts sounded a little far-fetched. Her legs were still bandaged under her prostheses because they had not yet completely healed. However, Joy was thrilled when presented with the idea of going skiing. She was aware that she was making unbelievable progress and gave God all the credit for her rapid improvements. Once the doctors gave us the green light, we were off looking forward to skiing once again and meeting other people who were sharing similar challenges.

I was thankful to be meeting these people. I had so many questions I wanted to ask about prostheses, like who is the very best prosthetist in the industry and how often does one need to get new prostheses? What about new technology and new materials for comfort and skin protection? What about liners and socks?

I was hoping to meet a mother who was an amputee so that I could ask her if it was difficult carrying a baby to full term because of the additional weight on her legs. I wanted to know how she managed to care for a new baby in the middle of the night. Did she first have to put on her leg(s)? For the fathers I wanted to know if they could still play games with their children in their yard. There were just so many unanswered questions in my mind that I was eager to meet every one of the amputees attending this ski event and hoped that they were open to sharing their lives and the answers to my questions.

Ken and I really did not expect Joy to ski much at all, but we were encouraged to know that there was special equipment for her should she be able to ski sometime in the future. One piece of equipment that impressed me was the outriggers, ski poles with little skis at the bottom that are intended to help balance the amputee skier.

Enthusiastically, Joy "suited up". Lessons were available to help orient the skier to the equipment and to the sport. Joy took to skiing as though she never left the slope. She had an incredible sense of balance and confidence. Equipped with outriggers to assist her, she skied down the mountain. The group attending this clinic consisted of mostly adult males, but there were a few children and their families. Everyone was having such a great time that I almost forgot to ask them my questions. Though I got many answered, seeing these amazing people get around and enjoying life was the most important thing.

Life did not seem complicated to them. Right now, these brave individuals were just having fun. They enjoyed life as though they weren't missing anything. What an inspiration they were to Ken, Tina, Joy and me. Watching one legged skiers hop around the lodge, or skiers with one arm grasp a ski pole tightly under the stump that was once their arm, and then heading down the slope fearlessly, I totally forgot that these guests were disabled.

At the end of the three-day ski clinic, the 52 Association/7-Eleven Amputee Ski Committee held downhill ski races. The races were not of a serious nature, but it was fun to cross the finish line feeling that rush of excitement and the thrill of competing even if it was just against the mountain. Gold medals were hung around the necks of all participants and each skier was given a certificate of accomplishment. As Ken, Tina and I cheered Joy across the finish line, we felt alive once again. Joy "won" two gold medals in the Supercap Slalom BK Race. BK meant bi-lateral, both legs, amputated below the knee. Joy won; however, she just happened to be the only BK competing in the race. Nevertheless, we were jumping up and down and cheering for her as though she had just won an Olympic gold medal. To us she had.

In these cherished moments of another of Joy's triumphant successes, we appeared to have smiles frozen on our faces from the cold wind that was blowing. But it was not the winter frost that kept the smiles on our faces; it was because we were witnessing the fulfillment of God's promise to Joy... "You will walk and run and play like other kids on false legs."

Photo at top right appeared in People Magazine
1982; bottom photo in People Magazine 1982
year-end edition. Photos courtesy of Marianne
Barcellona ©2009.

Chapter Twenty-Eight

God Will Help!

It was astonishing that Joy could ski. Her legs had not fully healed, were still bandaged under the liners of her prostheses and still resembled something she would never walk on again. Yet God's plan for Joy was much different from anything I could have dreamed or hoped for. He empowered her time and time again to do the impossible, even the unthinkable, like skiing down that slope. Where did she get the self-confidence to do these things? This confidence was not in herself — it was in God.

After our ski trip, I was excited to tell everyone about Joy, which I did repeatedly at the salon. Eyes wide open in amazement, my clients would listen intently to every detail, recollecting that only 10 months ago we were told that Joy was going to die and then that she was never going to walk again. I was sure to give credit to God every time for changing our circumstances from "impossible to overcome" to an astonishing victory.

Many clients nodded enthusiastically in agreement, others marveled and others just listened without a readable reaction. But all were supportive and thrilled for us. Soon, it became routine in the salon that clients or their friends who were suffering for almost any reason would ask me to help them comprehend the mystery of God and His willingness to help them in their time of crisis. One longtime client appeared unexpectedly in the salon immediately after her cancer diagnosis. She came to see me before even going home, so she could waste no time getting God involved. Still others came to be comforted after losing someone dear to them or for some encouragement facing difficult times with children or spouses.

One client, John, made a repeat visit. John was the resident who was at CHOP at the same time Joy was there, but who left CHOP when Joy was expected to die. John visited Creative Image Salon for a haircut shortly after Joy was released from the hospital. His disbelief at seeing Joy alive reminded us of just how close her brush with death really was.

John had moved south with his family, but he appeared on my schedule for a haircut. I asked him why he was in the area. Was he visiting here or had he moved back? His response was that he had left home very early that morning and had driven six hours just to talk to me. He didn't even need a haircut, but had made an appointment to make sure I had time to talk to him once he arrived.

John asked if we could talk someplace privately. The facial room was available and almost before the door was shut, John started talking. I listened intently as he poured out his heart about the events that were taking place in his life. His malpractice insurance had gone up so much that he feared he could not afford to continue practicing as an anesthesiologist. His anxiety was jeopardizing his marriage and family life and he was distressed and desperate for consolation and guidance. He continued, "I watched you for months in the hospital in a situation that was impossible to endure. However, you exhibited something through those months that was extraordinary. You know something about life and meeting difficult times and overcoming them that I now need to know."

I was humbled to think that my demeanor through this ordeal with Joy was exemplary in any way. I was more than thrilled to realize that John could see God working through me even though he did not identify these extraordinary attributes and powers as God. He asked me, "How did you do it?"

I replied, "I didn't. I couldn't have done it. It was impossible! The Lord did it."

He then asked timidly, "Will God help me?"

"Yes!" I replied with complete confidence. "God can and will bring hope, deliverance, guidance and peace even in difficult and impossible situations. And God is waiting for you to ask Him to help you."

"Will you tell me how to do that?" John asked.

I explained to him about the meaning of asking Christ into your heart and into your life. The best illustration I could think of was to compare us, even with our many talents and successes and ability to function in this world relatively well, to the first vans that came out. They were a very popular means of transportation, but soon their owners began converting these square boxes into highly functional vehicles. These conversions made the vans much more capable of meeting the owners' needs than ever imagined through the original design. Some owners raised the roofs for more headroom, some owners removed the back seats temporarily for extra cargo space, and some even used the van itself as a camper. The original van was good but not great. Conversion made the van extraordinary.

I continued my explanation by saying that this is exactly what God does to us. Once we invite Him into our lives, He takes something ordinary and converts it to something extraordinary. It is us plus God that makes life work extraordinarily better.

John still seemed confused about how to ask Christ into his heart. He wanted more explanation so I referred to John 3:16, which reminds us:

"For God so loved the world that He gave His only begotten Son.
That whoever believes in Him should not perish,
but have everlasting life."

I advised John to tell God that he loves Him and that he accepts His Son as the sacrifice for his sins. I suggested that John ask God to forgive him for anything he has done wrong, to set things right in his life, and to give him the strength to cope with these heartaches and fears. And to ask God directly for the money John needed to pay his malpractice and for the proper attitude and wisdom in dealing with his family right now. "Once you do these things, John," I added, "Ask God to give you the physical and emotional strength you need to cope with these things that are troubling you and the faith to know that God will take care of you."

I reminded John that asking God into his heart and into his life is a little like getting married. Saying, "I do" to God unites us together with God and makes us His children and members of His family, with all the benefits and promises and empowerment we need to solve life's problems and overcome life's challenges.

God says in Matthew 7:7 & 8:

"...Ask and it will be given to you; seek and you will find;
knock and it will be opened to you.
For everyone who asks receives;
and he who seeks finds; and to him who knocks,
it will be opened."

Quietly, I asked John, "Would you like to say 'I do' to God right now?"

We prayed together as John repeated after me these words of

acceptance:

> *"Dear Lord and Father, my God. I do acknowledge*
> *that You loved me enough to sacrifice Your son, Jesus,*
> *for payment of my wrongdoings that I might be forgiven*
> *and have eternal life.*
> *I do believe that Jesus is Lord*
> *and that You raised him from the dead.*
> *Please forgive me for all that I have done wrong in my life.*
> *I know You accept me just as I am, with all my faults, my guilt,*
> *and my shame. I do love You and I do need You in my life.*
> *Please take over my life*
> *and give me the joy, peace and hope only You can give.*
> *In Jesus' name, Amen."*

As John looked up, I could see that his brow, previously wrinkled with agony and frustration, now looked stress-free, his entire face appeared relaxed. John left the salon that day not feeling alone and despondent anymore, but hopeful and confident, not in himself, but in God.

Chapter Twenty-Nine

Joy in Being a Celebrity

Our lives remained pretty much the same for the next year. Then in the early part of 1984, a journalist from *People* magazine, Barbara Rowes, contacted us. Barbara had called Children's Hospital of Philadelphia inquiring about a potential story for the magazine. *People* magazine was not known for their medical stories, but rather for their stories about celebrities and famous people. CHOP told them about Joy, that she was skiing and suggested Ms. Rowes contact us, which she did.

We arranged for Barbara to visit with us so that we could share our story with her. After she interviewed us and decided to write the story, two photographers from the magazine came to take pictures of Joy at home with the family and then skiing at Jack Frost Mountain. One of the photographers, Marianne Barcellona, was particularly sensitive to Joy and took many keepsake pictures for her, especially one of Joy and her father embracing. The journalist and photographers were all wonderful people and instantly became good friends. It was interesting to me that they found Joy so fascinating. After all the people they had the privilege to meet, was Joy really that unusual?

We were certainly excited for Joy's story to be considered for *People* Magazine, but we were cautioned that the story could be "killed" (not run in the magazine) because it was a few years old and *People* magazine did not usually print medical stories. My response to Barbara, the journalist, was, "If God wants this story printed in your magazine, it will be printed." Barbara called me sometime afterwards to tell me not only would it be printed, but it would be four pages in the March 26, 1984, edition of *People* magazine. She told me when it would hit the newsstand in New York, and I drove up to meet her so that we could get first copies as they hit the stands. And there it was, a story marvelously told about a courageous little girl and her family. How delighted I was to realize that she was viewed as an inspiration to others.

After the magazine came out, we were invited to appear on *Hour Magazine* in California. The TV station paid for our trip to be on the show. While in California, we were also the guests of Warner Brothers Studio, since they represented Van Halen, Tina and Joy's favorite recording group as mentioned in the magazine article. While there, a local California newspaper assigned a reporter and photographer to us. They were going to run an article on Joy. As they were following us around various tourist spots that we were visiting as a family, Joy tripped going up a set of stairs and fell. All excited, the reporter and photographer hovered over her and almost pinned her on the ground where she had fallen to ask her, "Joy, what do you do when you fall down?" Joy politely pushed them aside so that she could get up and simply replied, "I get up. What do you do?"

Joy's popularity also brought about invitations to appear on other TV shows such as Baltimore's *People are Talking*, where we met Oprah Winfrey, who was the show's co-host at the time. As Oprah interviewed us, we were touched by the warmth and compassion in her voice as she spoke to Joy. At the year's end when *People* magazine published its issue of the 25 Most Intriguing People of 1984, Joy was one of those chosen. *Readers' Digest* also ran Joy's story in their January 1986 issue.

How exciting for Joy and our family to have been honored by these invitations to appear on television and to have so many articles written about her. Without question, Joy deserved to be admired, for she was tremendously courageous and inspiring, as well as blessed.

Joy and family
on the set of "Hour Magazine"— 1984

Chapter Thirty

Another Type of Crisis

While Joy was enjoying some recognition for returning to good health, we were facing another more private crisis. My husband, Ken, resumed his excessive drinking about six months after Joy came home from the hospital. His overindulgence in the past was often the cause for arguments and discontent between us. Maybe drinking was his way of coping with the physical, emotional and financial strain of Joy's illness, but it compounded what was already difficult for me.

From mid-1985 to mid-1986, I do not remember him ever coming home. Since two of our businesses were next to each other, I did occasionally see him when I was at the Mt. Holly salon and I did happen to know what bar he was "living" in. He routinely walked out the back door of the dry cleaners, sometimes in the early afternoon, crossed the back parking lot of the shopping center, and went into the back door of the bar, about 25 feet away from where he was working. He stayed at the bar until it closed and then slept in his truck or the drycleaners and repeated the same routine day after day.

I was not sympathetic towards him. I was the other person in this nightmare he was now creating! Although he occasionally interacted with us, it became obvious that the alcohol was replacing everything in his life. Christmas had been his time of year to shine. He had taught all of us how to enjoy the holiday. He was the best Santa ever. Generally we celebrated the holiday as a family on Christmas Eve.

When he stopped coming home for that, I think we all knew that he could not turn away from drinking. Maybe he was wishing for his own death to come. In reality, he was killing himself, slowly.

His alcoholism finally caused me to leave him in August of 1986. I took the girls and we temporarily moved into my Mother's townhouse because she and Pop were in Florida for the winter. Ken called me in September, shortly after I moved out, to tell me he had something stuck in his throat and was going to the doctor to have it removed. His doctor performed an endoscopy to remove the steak that had lodged deep in his throat and then the doctor examined Ken's esophagus and removed a small amount of tissue for a routine biopsy. We were shocked by the results of the biopsy: Ken was diagnosed with cancer of the esophagus and needed very extensive surgery or he would be dead in six months. Ken was not a strong person. Surgery, blood, and needles scared him to death. Whenever Joy got a needle, which was quite often, he had to leave the room. And this was going to be a BIG surgery for anyone! I returned to our home to care for him.

Since I was now the official "resident physician" of my family, I was ready to stay with him in the hospital. I had my hospital wardrobe ready to go. My family and I went to the hospital and waited almost eight hours until his surgery was over. Afterward he went to recovery and then to an ICU due to his condition and the severity of the surgery. Tina and Joy went home to stay with their grandparents, Mom and Pop.

The surgery itself was a success. Nevertheless, I chose to stay in the hospital with him. After all, I was an expert in this by now. What a terrible thing in which to become expert!

I also knew that God was in the hospital with us. He was not somewhere distant from my concerns. He was here. So together with His wisdom as to the outcome, I felt confident that we would make it through this. Nevertheless, when I saw Ken after surgery, he was distressed and extremely uncomfortable. I tried to talk to the nurse assigned to him, but she was not responding to my concerns. She seemed preoccupied with something and mechanically went about her job, and I was very worried that Ken's suffering would not be relieved if she were in charge of his care.

Even though I have the highest regard for the nursing profession and am forever grateful to the wonderful nurses who cared for Joy, I felt very uneasy about this particular nurse. Out of my concern for the situation I went to a quiet place to pray for Ken:

Lord, Ken is in a great deal of discomfort and pain and You know how difficult it is for him physically to endure this suffering. You made his body and You know of Ken's difficulty in coping with this surgery and the recovery from it. Nothing that is happening is a surprise to You. You, Lord have the ability to change every situation and solve every problem, so Lord, I ask that this evening You would provide someone to care for Ken who will be sensitive to his discomfort and his fears.
Father, surround him with people who are kindhearted and competent this night so Ken can sense their compassion and confidence and feel secure.
Also Lord, please bring about a solution for this nurse from whatever is troubling her this evening, that she may find peace and resolve coming from above.
And I thank You, Father, that I can come to You with all matters great or small that concern me, knowing that You hear my pleas and will answer according

to Your will. In Jesus' Name, Amen.

When I returned to Ken's side in the unit, another nurse had been assigned to him. His original nurse had been called to another floor. Some may think this was a coincidence, but I know differently. I have always believed that a coincidence is a small miracle in which God prefers to remain anonymous. In this case, I was most grateful and thanked God for answering my prayer. The new nurse was very compassionate and promptly got Ken's pain under control so he could rest comfortably. I am also confident that the nurse who was called to another floor found solutions that night for the matters that lay heavy on her heart.

After a ten-day stay in the hospital we went home and began what we hoped was recovery. The surgery was devastating to Ken physically, and the cancer had already begun to metastasize (spread) to other parts of his body, though we were not aware of this yet. A nurse friend had suggested Ken start drinking a high calorie protein supplement to bulk up, since he needed some reserve weight on him. He did do this, but now that the surgery was over and his anxiety had kicked in, he was not eating, and nourishment is quite necessary for healing. I suggested that we drive to Florida for a few weeks to my parents' home, which he absolutely loved, and he could recuperate in the warm weather and hopefully feel like eating.

While there, I went to a bookstore and bought a comprehensive book on cancer and started reading about Ken's type of cancer. Although my nurse friends had prepared me for the prognosis of his type of cancer as tenderly as they could, I needed more information. I needed to know what was ahead for us because I had to continue to run the businesses and our family. I felt I had to understand the demands that his illness would place on our family and me so that

I could accommodate them. Well, the information scared me to death! It was 1987 and according to the information available at that time concerning esophageal cancer, the disease was very quick spreading and the expected life span of the individual with this type of cancer was only months after the discovery of it. One month had already gone by. Ironically, hadn't we been told that unless Ken had this surgery he would be dead in six months? Then how many more months of life had he gained by having the surgery? I was alarmed! Here we go again, I thought!

Two weeks later when Ken seemed to be doing better, we returned home to New Jersey. One night as we were home watching TV, I discovered a lump on his neck. We immediately went back to the doctor. What was expected to happen with this cancer was happening; it had spread to his lymph nodes.

Although already compromised by the surgery and not yet fully recovered, he began chemotherapy. He was so weak that I would take cushions off the waiting room chairs in the doctor's office and place them on the wide windowsills for him to lie on. Next he was diagnosed with liver cancer, so radiation treatments began. We went to the hospital every day for six weeks for his radiation treatments.

He was getting extremely weak and the cancer had also spread to the bone and brain. We had come to realize that we could not win this battle but could be kept very busy coming to the hospital for treatments every day. Since his remaining days of life seemed to be dwindling, our daughters wanted to spend as much quality time with their Dad as possible, so we talked together about our plan for his last days.

We asked to talk to one of Ken's doctors with whom we really connected personally. We reviewed the types of cancer Ken now had and acknowledged that one of them was going to kill him. Our question was, wouldn't it make sense to choose the cancer that was least painful and let it run its course, rather than to eliminate a less painful cancer only for him to die a more painful death from another such as bone cancer? The doctor assured us that as the end drew near, the brain cancer would make him sleep and later make him comatose. Yet, for a few weeks at least, he would be mobile, alert and at home with us. Remember, Ken was not heroic in suffering, so having this choice seemed compassionate. The doctor agreed and with kindness and sadness for us all, he dismissed us to return home until the end came.

Chapter Thirty-One

A Sad Farewell

One early morning in March 1987, Ken awakened me to tell me what he had just experienced. He said that he did not know how long this experience lasted, but that he awoke to see Jesus standing in the corner of our bedroom with his hands outstretched to him. He then saw a review of his entire life. And as his life passed before him, he did not feel uncomfortable or guilty for all the things he had done. This life review was not for the sake of judgment. In fact, he felt forgiven and hopeful of entering his eternal life. Afterwards, Ken began to live with purpose and confidence for the first time in his life. He went to visit his mother in the nursing home to tell her that he was going to die but that he was resigned to it. He exhibited wisdom uncommon to him or most individuals looking directly in the face of death.

He decided to drive to Florida in his most prized possession, his Corvette. Joy, now 11 years old, asked to go along. Even though she was in school, we made the decision for her to accompany her father on his final trip to Florida. With the remaining days in Ken's life so few, we chose not to hang on to routine for the sake of it. We listened instead to our hearts. Joy could go to school another day, but spending time with her Dad in these final months was an irreplaceable opportunity. Florida for Ken was a refuge. My Mother and Pop were there and wanted to help take care of him.

After the road trip with her father and a week in Florida, Joy flew home. Ken remained. What I did not know at the time was that he planned to stay there until he died. Nevertheless, since I talked to him regularly, I could hear in his voice that he was failing. I flew down to bring him home and to drive his car back. Actually, I believe he would have liked his car buried with him. That's how much he worshipped it.

It was an amazingly long ride home. A trip that usually took two days was going to take us four. I drove, of course. We had to stop every few hours because Ken would have to get out of the car, lie on the grass for about a half hour at the side of the road to rest because of the pain he was suffering and then we would resume the trip. When we arrived home, I immediately took Ken back to the hospital to insist that the pain medication be increased.

That same night while we were watching TV as a family, I noticed that Ken was pulling at one ear and then another as he was sticking out his tongue and making funny faces. It was humorous. I asked him how he was feeling and if he had any pain. He replied that for the first time in months he did not have any pain. "In fact," he joked, "I feel so good right now that when it's my time to go, I'm not going."

But these days there was much to be serious about and Ken's time to go would come soon enough. My children were losing their father. Sadness and purpose engulfed our home. We just wanted to be home together as the moments ticked by. But my mother had a different theory as to how waiting for the end should be done. After all, she had experienced death occurring in the home since she was a young girl. So she called my brother and his family and my sister and her husband and insisted that they come as soon as possible to our house to provide companionship and comfort to us. She also decided that during this process we needed to eat.

Now as much as I like to eat, I do not have to eat at any regular time. But Mom decided we needed to eat a good sit-down meal. So from the kitchen she came into the living room to ask me about the turkey breast that was in the freezer and whether she should cook it. I didn't care! My focus and interest was on Ken and his last moments of life, but Mom figured we had to eat sometime too. So she persisted in her questioning about the turkey breast. It was a conversation I did not need to have at the time and I have often thought about it. My mother's intentions were good, but she should have just proceeded with what she knew had to be done without engaging me in the conversation.

She and my sister-in-law cooked the turkey breast and made dinner and I did appreciate eating a good meal, but my mind was on my daughters and how they would be after their father passed away. They had already been through so much in their short lives. However, having a good meal at this time made me realize years later that friends and family should do for people in tragic situations what they see is needed.

Astonishingly, Ken kept hanging onto life. I could not figure out what else needed to be accomplished in order for him to let go. We had called his family to come to say good-bye. Even our daughters said good-bye, which was extremely difficult. One evening I could not understand why he was not letting go. All signs for his life to end were there. I took the girls aside and talked to them about saying good-bye to their Dad again, one at a time. I specifically remember Tina's remarks to her Dad. Tearfully she told him that she understood how sick he was and that he wasn't going to live much longer. She told him how much she would miss him when she graduated from high school (she was a junior) and that when she got married, she would be sad that he would not be there to walk her down the aisle. These comments were very honest and very touching. Her father turned to her and said, "Tina, whenever you want me, just look high into the sky for the brightest star. That will be me looking down on you."

Even still he clung to life. The girls and I had been sleeping in the living room with him. He was in a hospital bed, I was on the couch, and the girls were in their sleeping bags on the floor. He was very weak. One night a light went on in my head. I realized that he did not want to die in front of his children. I sent the girls to bed, saying that I would take care of Daddy and that they should get a good night's rest in their own beds. He died just a few hours after they went to bed. It was April 17, 1987; he was only 46.

After the nurse, Brenda, a dear friend, and I bathed Ken and put fresh pajamas on him, changed the bed, then combed his hair, I went upstairs to wake the girls. I went to get Tina and Joy so they could come back down stairs to say their good-byes to their father once again. As I got to the top of the stairs, which was almost directly in line with Tina's room, she sat up to greet me as though she knew I was coming.

A few months after Ken's death, we were at the shore with our family sitting around playing a game of questions. It was Tina's turn and her question was, "Have you ever had a strange dream and what was it?" Tina acknowledged that she had experienced a strange dream, but being the private person that she is, she would not divulge the dream.

Later that evening, privately, I asked her about her dream. She asked me if I remembered that she had sat straight up in her bed the night Daddy died and I came up to tell her. I, of course, remembered that. I thought it was strange but dismissed it with very little thought because so much else was going on. She then told me that she had a "dream," a vision that night. She said she saw what was going on down in the living room in her sleep and knew that her father had died. In fact he spoke to her. He said, "Tina, you and Joy will be fine. Your mother is strong." I told her that I did not believe this to be a dream, but rather that her spiritual eyes had been opened, which allowed her to see his last moments of life and that her father spoke to her on his way to heaven. How special that was for her!

Joy and her father

Photo courtesy of Marianne Barcellona ©2004

Chapter Thirty-Two

A Widow at 39

A widow at 39? Here I was, a single mom with two children to support, three businesses to run and deeply in debt. No matter how dismal things seemed though, we still had a roof over our heads (mainly because my mother held the mortgage on our home). And the businesses were still operating. The credit for the continuation and success of the businesses really goes to the employees. They were not just hardworking, but extremely supportive of our ongoing problems.

Our clients, too, understood the situation and, despite the many times I was out of the salon for one reason or another, they remained loyal. I don't know if they had any idea how much I needed their business, but I did! What an amazing group of compassionate people they were back then and continue to be even in my current salon. Until people have a loved one with a medical need in their home, they have no idea how costly in time, effort and money it is. There were years when Joy's medical and affiliated medical needs cost more than I could possibly earn. When she was in need, I was with her. I was fortunate to have the energy to work long hours when I did return. I couldn't live on a budget projected for tomorrow's expenses and needs; I was always paying off yesterday's and last year's debts. Thank God I was self-employed. What employer would put up with me?

I was not afraid to be "alone." Sometimes, I had felt alone in my marriage. This new feeling of "alone" I could understand. Ken had died. I was alone to raise my children and earn a living. I mentioned to a friend attending Ken's funeral how I felt I had this new responsibility for the girls and for the businesses.

He immediately brought me back to reality by saying, "It has been all up to you for quite a while. This is not a new situation for you."

I thought, "So much for feeling sorry for myself. My friend is right! Now, Karen, just get on with it."

Although Ken had given me reason to feel distant from him, I had no doubt that God loved him and forgave him and that Ken was in heaven; I had been present the day Ken accepted Christ as his Savior. Life tormented Ken, but I was sure that eternity, through his faith in Jesus Christ, had brought him the peace he had been longing for.

That night after the funeral when the girls were in bed asleep, I just wanted to talk to my Friend and tell Him how sad this day was for us and ask Him to continue to be with my daughters and me through this new journey that was ahead for us, so I prayed:

Lord, thank You for Your promise of eternal life. I know that even at this moment Ken is with You; and all the things that were confusing and disturbing to him in this life are now gone and he is enjoying being in Your presence and sharing in the glory of heaven.
Thank You for the truth of Your word as You told us in Matthew 5: 12:
"Rejoice and be glad, because great is your reward in heaven."
So today, Father, even through my sadness, I rejoice knowing that Ken is no longer suffering and that You have already rewarded him with a new perfect body free of pain and disease.
And Lord, thank You for our wonderful family and great friends and for all the many kindnesses they showed us today.
Their presence alone lifted us up above our sorrow.

Father, there are days ahead that are uncertain for me. I will now have the full responsibility of raising the girls and caring for them as they grow into young women. And right now I am concerned for them because they are broken hearted by the loss of their father who loved them, but can no longer be here with them. Help them overcome their enormous grief.

Since I had a life of my own before I married Ken, I know that I will be ok now, but our daughters have never experienced life without their father and they do not have that same assurance of their lives being ok without him.

Comfort them, Father with your presence, especially this evening of their father's funeral, that they will feel assured that although their earthly father has left them, their Heavenly Father will never leave them.

Lord, help me be a good parent and an understanding one. Help me guide them into their futures holding on to them to protect them when necessary, but knowing when to let go so that they can learn to stand boldly on their own.

Help me instill in my daughters Your values and principles that we may be a family of faith, love, forgiveness, laughter and truthfulness.

Father, make clear your plan for our lives. Direct and guide us that we may be able to clearly see Your hand in each decision we make that we may walk with You, not ahead of You and never behind You for we might miss the blessings and opportunities because of our own hesitations and insecurities. Lord, give us courage to place our lives in Your hands so that at the appropriate time, we will be able to move forward to the next step of our lives' journeys knowing that You have led us there.

Thank You, Lord, for the businesses and the people who

work in them. Thank You for the income the businesses have provided for us. Make me a good steward of these gifts of income that I might show You how thankful I am for the blessings we have received as a family from our businesses.

Lord, You know what is facing me tomorrow when I go to work. I have many employees and many responsibilities and many debts. Help me, Lord, to be effective, confident and sincere in meeting all of my obligations.

Lord, help me be a good manager of people and resources that I may direct with purpose and persistence and succeed in my commitment to provide for my family and my staffs' families.

Lord, help us begin tomorrow afresh in spirit and renewed in strength to meet the challenges and the blessings that will come with each new day. Grant us rest, Lord, and please help Tina, Joy and me remember that everything we have came from You and that no matter what the future holds for us-You will always be our loving, faithful friend on whom we can depend. In your Heavenly Name and with Thanksgiving, Amen.

§§§

One thing that Ken and I had done as a young married couple was to make sure that our affairs were in order. Our wills stated that upon the death of either spouse, the remaining spouse would inherit everything. We were the beneficiaries on each others' life insurance policies also. Even though the death benefit was not much, the benefits would be enough to help the surviving spouse start a new life or sustain the present one. If we were both killed in an accident, everything would then be equally divided between the girls. We did not know when death would come for either of us, but we did the responsible thing in planning and providing for each other and our children. As a result, his death was not as financially devastating as it could have been.

Everyone says that a widow should not make any big decisions for a year after her spouse dies, but only four months after Ken's death a piece of property came up for sale that seemed like a perfect new "home" for the salon in Moorestown. I had been paying rent in all the buildings that housed the businesses and was tired of doing that. This property and the modest insurance benefit presented the opportunity to get away from paying rent for the salon in Moorestown. It also fit our image. It was a lovely, quaint 2 1/2-story house that backed up to the municipal parking lot. I had done some consulting work in our industry through East Coast Salon Services and had once consulted for a salon that was in a house converted to a beauty salon. I liked how the home-like environment welcomed and even embraced the clients. I hoped one day to buy such a home, and this one fit the description and was in the exact location I had been waiting for.

The idea for a location for a new salon was just one of the many ways East Coast Salon Services helped me and many other salon owners. Although the company excelled in sales of products and in customer service to salons, East Coast Salon Services was committed to empowering owners of even the smallest salons to be the best they could be. Stan Klet and Joe Marcelli, the principals of the company, mentored me and provided me education in new trends, techniques and business practices in the beauty industry. It was through my association with them and their willingness to believe in me that I grew professionally. Eventually Stan and Joe gave me the opportunity to teach other stylists and salon owners. As a result, my staff and I could be "on the cutting edge" of information and styles and I could gain some valuable experience in public speaking. My association with East Coast Salon Services is the single most important ingredient in my success within the industry and gave me the courage to pursue this much larger home for my salon.

Joy enjoying the beach

Chapter Thirty-Three

A New Beginning

This building, 117 North Church Street in Moorestown, had my name on it, I was sure of it. This would be the perfect spot for a new home for Creative Image Salon and would eventually accommodate a day spa as the business expanded. I made an offer. After a counter offer and a bit more haggling, the seller and I agreed to sign an agreement of sale, but I first wanted to consult our family attorney to review it.

Mr. Lawrence Eleuteri, Esq., our attorney, had been my parents' attorney for many years and had helped them through any issues that arose from their own small business. By the way my mother raved about him, we thought he must walk on water. "He is such a gentleman," she would sigh. "He's just so soft spoken, with a kind manner about him, yet so knowledgeable." My mother was not easily impressed, but clearly this man was high on her list. Though she thought lawyers in general were controlling and argumentative, to her, this Mr. Eleuteri was different. Every time she returned from his office, I would hear about how wonderful he was.

True, Mr. Eleuteri had impressive educational and legal credentials. A graduate of University of Notre Dame and Georgetown Law Center, he was senior partner of his own firm and had practiced law in the county for over 20 years. At my parents' suggestion, Ken and I had hired Mr. Eleuteri in 1987 to help us revise our wills. Because of Ken's illness and weakened condition, Mr. Eleuteri very kindly brought the new wills to our house for us to sign. When Mr. Eleuteri saw how ill Ken was, he was obviously deeply moved. He himself had lost his wife to cancer a few years earlier. As Ken was signing his will, I thought I saw Mr. Eleuteri wiping something from his eye, a tear perhaps.

Now, four months after Ken's death, when I was ready to sign the agreement of sale for the new salon, I called Mr. Eleuteri to ask him to review the agreement the next day. Instead, he suggested he meet me at the salon that same night and accompany me to the real estate agency to review the agreement of sale. I really did not think I needed him to go along, but I decided it couldn't hurt to have an attorney present. When he got out of his car, I remembered one thing I did not like about him — his haircut. It was a $3 special. I couldn't walk down the street of my hometown with somebody who had a haircut like that. After all, I am a hairstylist! So I dragged him into the salon and convinced him to allow me to cut his hair. He was a bit resistant and told me he had never been in a beauty salon before. "Well," I thought, "there's a first time for everything."

The agreement was fine, but the building was a residence and I would need variances from the township planning and/or zoning boards before it could be occupied as a salon. Mr. Eleuteri knew just how to handle these matters. We had to appear before the local boards. The evening came when my application would be discussed before the board. Since Mr. Eleuteri was accompanying me as my attorney, he reassured me he would do all the talking. "Oh, no you won't," I replied sternly. "Nobody talks for me. This is my industry and I will do the talking. I know what I need from the township to make this business successful in this building." So Mr. Eleuteri sat quietly as I did the talking. I had no clue that the lawyer was supposed to be the one to do the talking, and I was supposed to be the one to sit quietly. Nevertheless, Mr. Eleuteri politely complied with my unusual request. We got through meeting one.

After the next month's meeting when my application seemed likely to be approved by the board, Mr. Eleuteri, now Larry to me, suggested we celebrate with a drink after the meeting. We went to a nearby restaurant that had a rather nice bar area. We talked about my application and the process and the excitement of remodeling the house for the salon.

I had a cold and sniffled the whole time, but in between sniffles I discovered that Larry was such a devoted father that he cooked dinner every night for his three children. He had even declined an interview for a very prestigious position as a bankruptcy judge so he could spend more time with and be there for his children.

October was the month the annual hospital ball was held. I was on the committee for the ball, so even though I was a recent widow, I felt I should go. And I sincerely wanted to support this hospital any way possible since the medical and hospital staffs were so supportive during Joy's crises. These people were dear friends and this hospital was very important to me.

So, whom would I ask to the ball? It occurred to me that the lawyer, Larry Eleuteri, would make a nice impression. Even though he was almost 18 years older than I, he had a full head of gray hair and, especially with more stylish haircuts, he looked very distinguished.

I instantly called him at his office and blurted out. "Would you like to go to the hospital ball with me?"

"Yes," he replied, sounding very serious and formal, yet with just a slight hint of excitement.

I got a bit nervier and asked, "Can you dance?"

"A little," he said.

I assumed that meant that he couldn't dance. After all, he's a lawyer. Not wanting to offend him, but also wanting to know if he could really dance, I gently suggested we go out dancing sometime before the ball. So we made a date for the next Saturday night and we went dancing at a nearby ballroom. In my generation, what I thought was dancing was just jumping around to one's own beat as your partner did the same. But in Larry's generation, couples danced together— the waltz, the fox trot, the jitter-bug, the rumba; and he was an amazingly fabulous dancer. I then discovered that as a youth, he belonged to a young Catholic group that went dancing every Saturday night. Well, it was I who was embarrassed. I was the one who could not dance—certainly not at all like Larry. I was finding this lawyer very interesting and sociable, not boring at all.

I had myself a date for the ball! This was all new to me, this dating thing. I had been married for 17 years. Larry couldn't have been a more perfect man, but I was not looking for a relationship. All I needed was a date for the ball.

My building variances had not all been approved yet, so Larry and I continued to see each other at the township meetings where he continued to represent my interests. One day, though, he called to ask me out to dinner. The ball was just around the corner, so I thought it would be nice to continue getting to know him. He was easy to talk to and to admire, so sincere with absolutely no pretense about him. He was also so dedicated to his family — something I had not experienced in my own marriage. I understood why my mother thought so highly of him. She couldn't believe I was going out with Mr. Eleuteri; I couldn't believe it either.

Our interest in each other grew, much to my surprise. For me, it was especially nice to know a man who was totally grown up with no hang-ups, no addictions, no insecurities and the same Christian foundation for living. This man knew how to be in a loving, committed relationship. But I was nervous! Our friendship was moving very quickly, and I still harbored some fears from my past relationship. I knew I could depend on myself, but I did not have the experience of sharing life's journey with someone who was going in the same direction. I also was aware that I had developed some assertive traits during my marriage. I was independent, outspoken, driven, focused, bold and matter of fact. What did this man see in me?

However, God had a different plan for my life and Larry seemed to be a big part of it. To make sense out of confusion, I took a piece of paper and systematically and logically started two columns, "the pros and the cons of Larry." I could not depend on my own emotions and I was beginning to feel attracted to him. I had been betrayed by my emotions once, and I did not fully believe I was ready for another relationship. The "Pro" column was full of everything I ever wanted in a soul mate; the "Con" column had only two items: I didn't like the way he generally wore his hair and I didn't care for his choice of suits. "Good heavens," I thought, "What am I thinking? Those two things can easily be changed!"

Creative Image Salon & Day Spa

Chapter Thirty-Four

The Judge and The Mayor

By November of 1987, Larry and I realized that we were in a serious relationship. Larry was not the kind of man who was going to have a long-term relationship outside of marriage. I, however, thought we could date for years. But in his wisdom Larry explained to me, "Right now, I am excited to come over to see you and you are excited to see me, but as time passes, I will be too tired to come over and you will be too tired to see me. The relationship will drift apart and sooner or later, there will be no relationship. When you fall in love, you set a date to be married. You keep the relationship intact and moving forward." What a refreshing difference from the thinking of my generation, I thought.

We decided to wait to get married until July 10, 1988, as our children did not even know each other. With this romance of ours moving so quickly, I'm not sure they had time to digest the fact that their parents were getting re-married…and we would all be moving in together. Our new blended family would consist of: Joy (12), Tina (17), and Larry's children, Robert, known to all as Rob, (16), Gloria, affectionately called Glor (21), and Lawrence Jr., referred to as Lar (22). I sold the homestead and moved to Cinnaminson because Larry had been elected to the township committee in that town. Obviously, he could not move out of town and still serve on the township committee, so I was the one who chose to move.

Together we bought a wonderful 85-year-old Georgian-style

home with enough bedrooms and common space to accommodate our blended family. The size of the property surrounding the house was another important consideration since three of our children had cars and along with the two cars Larry and I owned, a considerable amount of off-street parking was necessary. I was also enamored with the charming little guest house that was on the property, thinking that at some time, my mother and Pop would be its occupants. I was comfortable that our new "nest" would provide the right sense of home and family. We both were aware that there would be some rough spots to work out with five children who barely knew each other, but the house was perfect for us to begin afresh as a family.

What I hadn't calculated was my new role of the cook for seven people every night. One day over lunch, before Larry and I got married, I told him very seriously, even sternly, that I did not cook every night. "Okay." he said, probably thinking how naïve I was to think that could still be true with so many people to feed, but he went along. We prepared at least five pounds of meat, five pounds of potatoes along with vegetables and salad each night. Friday night was pizza night and I did not cook. I wouldn't change that for anything! When the girls and I lived by ourselves, we ate out almost every night, but it's far too expensive to order out or eat out with seven people at the table. Although I did most of the cooking, Larry did his share too. Cooking regularly — and for this number of people — was a big adjustment for me.

And then in 1990, Mom and Pop moved into our guesthouse as I had hoped would happen one day. Mom had diabetes and was having problems with circulation in her feet. In fact, she had fallen down the steps in her townhouse and knew it was time to move to a one-floor home. When she came to our house to tell me she was moving into a nursing home, I was shocked because I knew she hated the idea of living in a nursing home. I picked up on the vague hint she was throwing, and thank God I did. "Mom," I said, "When Larry and I bought this property with the guest house on it, I thought if you ever needed to move to a one-story house, you would consider living here." Mom immediately began telling me her thoughts on what she needed done to the house for her and Pop to live there. I was amused at her well-thought-out plan. Obviously it had been on her mind for a while.

With Mom and Pop joining us for dinner most nights, the number at the dinner table was now nine. Larry had always known the importance of eating together as a family, and I learned to accept it as necessary. But I went kicking and screaming each day to the kitchen to perform my new duties. Most nights after work, I would enter the house through the kitchen door, put my handbag down and start cooking without changing my clothes or shoes or sitting down for even a brief pause. A few times I thought I would take the long way home, maybe stop for a soda, hoping that when I arrived home everyone would have had peanut butter and jelly sandwiches or something to eat so that I did not have to cook. This never happened. Instead, each night, all eight were waiting for me to cook. Although I cooked grudgingly, Larry was so considerate of everything I had to do and every place I had to be, that I soon adjusted to cooking and preserving the sanctity of the family's evening meal.

Since Larry was on the township committee, I also got involved with the various campaigns and fundraisers. It was great for us to be involved in something together. Working in local politics gave me a sense of the town and helped me meet new people. I was surprised I became interested in politics. Before I married Larry, I'm not sure I even knew who the President of the United States was. Then in 1990, Larry became the Mayor. In our town the mayor is not elected by the people but "elected" by the township committee. The term is for one year, then rotates among the other members of the committee. As Mayor he was invited to many events and I accompanied him. It was exciting. I was really settling in to the community and enjoying my new life with my husband.

Then in 1991 Larry was appointed to the bench. No one was ever more deserving or more suited to the high standards of the New Jersey judiciary than Larry. Although he had very humble beginnings as a young boy from Bordentown, New Jersey, his mother and stepfather provided a comfortable home for him and his older sister, Madeline, filled with love and devotion. Their Catholic faith and Catholic education taught them discipline and humility and, thanks to their mother's determination to overcome adversity, their lives were complete although without privilege. However, through God's plan for Larry's life, a man with great character and wisdom was being formed through these early years. He empathized with those who came before him on the bench. He understood the lives and trials and sufferings of the common person as he was one himself. Here was truly a man who was loved and respected by his family and recognized within his profession as an exceptional individual and brilliant attorney.

His journey as an adult began after high school. He joined the Naval Reserves. He was working full time at Beverly National Cemetery when he was called into active duty because of the Korean War. He began attending Rider College at night while stationed at Lakehurst Naval Air Station in Lakehurst, New Jersey. The war came to an end, as did his Naval career, and he began looking at transferring to another college. With the GI bill, and a good nudge from his supply officer, he applied to the University of Notre Dame. Dressed in his navy blues and flying to South Bend by Navy transport, he made his way to the campus of his heart's dreams. That day, he found out that he had been accepted to this great university. The American dream for one more boy from this great country came true.

After graduating from college, Larry took a job as an auditor with a national accounting firm. Soon he discovered that his real interest was in law. So in the fall of 1959, he set off for Georgetown Law Center in Washington, D.C. He returned home after graduation to marry and to practice law. Eventually he was the senior partner in his own firm. Then later, after years of experience, he became a judge. His mother, of course, attended the ceremony. This woman, who was one of six children whose parents immigrated to this country from Perugia, Italy, and who never finished the eighth grade herself, had the privilege of witnessing her son being sworn in as a Superior Court Judge. There was never a more proud mother than she on this day. Clearly she had instilled in her children the confidence and motivation it takes to succeed. Sadly, she passed away in 2001 at the age of 92. I am fortunate to have known such an amazing woman.

Prior to going on the bench, Larry had to resign from the township committee. It was then that I became interested in serving in local government. I was appointed to the Planning Board and became president of our local Republican Club. Shortly thereafter, I was asked to become president of a county Republican woman's organization, which I accepted.

New Jersey was soon to elect its first woman governor and those of us who wanted to make a difference for women joined her campaign. With her victory the glass ceiling for women in New Jersey had finally been broken. As president of the county organization, I received calls from all over the state requesting names of women from Burlington County who could be considered for appointments to various state boards. In 1994 I was asked to run for township committee. I won the election and was delighted to be representing the people of Cinnaminson and in 1997, I became the Mayor of Cinnaminson. I was honored to be assisting in the framing of ordinances and sincere in my attempt to positively affect the lives of the residents of Cinnaminson. My thinking and actions, my philosophies and my convictions were now being molded into a part of the history of our town. I took this very seriously and began to examine my own core values. These were exciting times for me and for the women of New Jersey.

The Judge and the Mayor

Chapter Thirty-Five

Joy's Victory

Joy's years in Junior High were almost normal, but never uneventful. Even though we had moved to Cinnaminson, Joy attended school in Moorestown where she had grown up. When other kids were going to the nurse because they needed some medical assistance, Joy was going to the janitor to use his screwdriver to reattach her foot. One day as she was sitting with her legs crossed, unknown to her, her foot came loose and turned completely backwards. The student sitting next to her who saw this happen let out a very loud screech. He apparently didn't know about Joy. "Does anyone have a screwdriver?" Joy asked with a smile.

Sometimes if her leg was "bothering" her, she would take it off and rest her stump on the top of the desk.

Another challenge was buying shoes. The feet of the prostheses are wide and large and the shoes themselves need rubber soles so that Joy wouldn't slip. One day Joy, Tina, my cousin. Maureen Fowler, and I went shopping for shoes for Joy. Maureen was always protective of Joy and sensitive to her physical appearance. Maureen, a beauty herself and always very well dressed, wanted Joy to make a fashion statement with her sneakers. Once the saleswoman brought shoes for Joy to try on, Maureen took over. Tina and I just sat and watched while Maureen, all dolled up, got down on her knees on the floor to help Joy try on the shoes. It's not easy to force a rubber foot into a shoe, but Maureen didn't give up easily. She pushed and shoved until Joy's feet went into the shoe.

Next Maureen proceeded to make sure the shoes were comfortable for Joy. She methodically pressed down on the front of each shoe at the toe like women have always done for children, asking Joy if she had enough room in each shoe, did they feel comfortable and did the shoes hurt her feet? Almost immediately, Maureen realized what she was doing and how ridiculous the questions were that she was asking Joy. Maureen raised her head and looked at Joy ready to apologize for offending her when Maureen was met with a burst of laughter from Joy, Tina and myself. Being the fashion coordinator that she is, Maureen suddenly realized that Joy could enjoy buying shoes merely for fashion and did not have to consider fit and comfort. We left the store that day with the best looking shoes the store had to offer thanks to Maureen. Mission accomplished!

Once I was very late to a doctor's appointment for Joy and was speeding down a major highway. Out of nowhere came a police car with its lights flashing, signaling me to pull over. I turned to Joy, who was sitting next to me in the passenger's seat and said, "Take off your legs and set them next to you on the seat — quickly!" She did. When the officer looked in the window to talk to me, he hardly could take his eyes off the pair of legs sitting on the seat next to Joy. He then looked at Joy and realized that she had no legs. The shocked look on his face let me know that I probably would not get a ticket this time. He warned me to slow down and permitted us to continue on our way.

Although there were many funny stories to share through those years, the next turn in the road for Joy, adolescence, brought many disappointments and heartaches. Joy was now in high school and had reached her mature height and weight. Her "little" leg could no longer support her adult frame. She couldn't bear any weight on the end of her stump and there was not enough subcutaneous tissue around the bottom for the prosthesis to be held in place when she walked. Joy accepted herself as she was but had one rule. She would not go to school in a wheel chair. In fact she almost never used a wheel chair. Walking meant everything to her, and now her short leg couldn't support any weight. The end of the stump was so small and bony it was like walking on her elbow. Impossible. She was 16, a time in a young girl's life when friends, school and having a social life means everything, but she was missing out on it all. As her mother, it was becoming harder and harder to make her life a happy one. When she was just a little child I could buy her an ice cream cone and it would put a smile on her face. Nothing I could do now would bring a smile.

As we searched for answers to the problem with her short leg, her orthopedic doctor, Dr. Dennis Drummond, told us she needed a "free-flap" transfer. By transplanting a muscle from somewhere else on Joy's body to the bottom of her stump, surgeons hoped to provide her with the weight bearing cushion her "little leg" needed to bear her weight. If it worked.

As we searched our regional hospitals for the right physician to do this very delicate procedure, we heard the name of a doctor in Louisville, Kentucky, mentioned as the best in this specialty, Dr. Joseph Banis. We were told he had done amazing reconstructions on people using flaps. We made an appointment with that doctor and off Joy, Tina and I went to Kentucky. I am always surprised that people select a hospital or a doctor that is 10 miles closer to home than another. I could never let distance dictate; it is results that I was after. It was well worth the sacrifice to go wherever we would get the best results. For us we were hoping it was Kentucky.

Dr. Banis had never seen anyone with Joy's condition before.

This was not unusual considering the rarity of the disease and the mortality rate of over 90%. Yet Dr. Banis said he felt sure the free-flap surgery could be done for someone like her. We liked his manner and his confidence. Our first opinion by a doctor stated only a 25% chance of success. This percent was not high enough to put her through this long surgery or to have her donate another portion of her body only to have it slough off. The free-flap that was going to be used for Joy was the large muscle in the inner portion of the leg starting at the groin and extending down to the knee. When we asked Dr. Banis what he thought she would be able to do after this surgery, he asked, "What did she do up to this point?" We said she did everything. Dr. Banis' response was, "Then that's what she'll do again." We knew we were in the right place. She was going to walk again!

With all our years of hands-on medical and hospital experience, we knew how to quickly recognize the physician who was extraordinary in his/her specialty. In our experiences, an extraordinary physician, or any individual possessing extraordinary skills, does not flinch when presented with a problem, but after purposeful deliberation, moves forward towards the solution with confidence. Recognizing these attributes in Dr. Banis, a vascular surgeon, we made a commitment to the surgery for Joy. Joy was expected to be in the hospital for about five weeks following the surgery, so once again, I packed our hospital wardrobes and other essentials and Larry, Joy and I headed south to Kentucky.

Joy was in surgery for what seemed like an eternity - more than eight hours. This vascular surgery involved the time consuming process of delicately suturing dozens of tiny veins together. During a long procedure, such as Joy's, the anesthesiologist periodically brings the patient out of a deep sleep to a higher level of consciousness and then back into a deep sleep. When the surgery was done and Joy was being wheeled back to her room, her screams could be heard all the way down the hall. Larry said chills ran up his spine from her shrieks. Where was she? How could I get to her? I must get to her! I arrived at her room at just the same time as her stretcher. She literally seemed frightened to death. She had experienced anesthesia recall. When the anesthesiologist brought her up to near consciousness, Joy could feel some of the surgical procedures but could not speak. In her mind she was screaming for help, but no one could hear her. She was scared to death. But she did not give up. Once again, she fought to live.

As her mother, I had made the decision to fight to keep her alive when she was a little girl who was dying from a complication of the chicken pox. She trusted me. She allowed me to fight for her. I often questioned whether I was right. She was only a child then and respected my decision, but how about now that she was a young woman? I often wondered if she thought it was the right thing to save her life now that she was older and was living the life of a disabled young girl and would someday be a disabled woman. Was she still glad to be alive? Death is sometimes the correct choice. Her death would have been very difficult for us at the time, but would it have been easier for her? I wasn't so naïve as to think that once we got home from the hospital in 1982 that our lives would be without complications. I was entirely committed to her living a quality life through her entire life. Whatever it took. My commitment to her went from the day she was born to the day I die. And it became an even greater commitment on my part to both my children when I realized that I could actually lose one of them.

But, I wondered if she felt that her life, the way it was, with the suffering that she had to go through year after year, day after day, was worth living. Was she glad to be alive? She was 16 now. We didn't know anyone else like her. She was physically challenged which made her appear different, but she was special in many other ways as well. She was persistent, self-confident, and courageous and always maintained an inherent positive attitude. But were these qualities enough to justify the pain and the struggles to keep Joy going on? Given the choice all over again, would she, herself, fight to stay alive? I needed to know the answer to that question. Although I would not ever want her to experience any more pain or fear, this day, in Louisville, I had the answer to a question I had been asking myself for years. And, thank God the answer was YES! I now knew that she would fight for her own life. Scared and frightened out of her mind, she would not give in to death. This day, she made the decision herself to live out her life with her disfigurement and her disability.

Once again, right after the surgery, she experienced a temperature of 106 degrees. The surgeons took her back in the OR to debriede her and then her temperature went down. After that brief episode, recovery went as expected. However, we were told to be prepared for the doctors to attach live leaches to her should infection set in. The leaches would eat away the infection. Thank God that wasn't necessary.

The doctors in Louisville were astounded at Joy's ability to recover after surgery. She always wanted to eat immediately afterwards. They were surprised to discover that she actually could. One day, after a procedure, as I was waiting near the recovery room for someone to tell me her surgery was finished, the recovery room door swung open and out came Joy on the OR stretcher with the surgeon and the anesthesiologist pushing her. They took her directly to the fast food restaurant in the hospital from the recovery room for something to eat. Joy was amazing in many ways. Survival was her game.

Chapter Thirty-Six

Drugs: the Enemy

Joy's high school years in Moorestown Senior High School started off with great promise. Even though she began missing a great deal of school because of problems with her short leg, she was elected class vice-president in her freshman and sophomore years. But, since her surgery in Louisville during her sophomore year, she had missed so much school and was on home-bound instruction so much of the time, that the Moorestown school district informed us that they would no longer accept Joy as an out of district student.

Not being permitted to stay in school with the friends she had known since kindergarten was a blow too difficult for her to overcome, and this rejection brought about a new low for her. She seemed to lose interest in many things. She dutifully transferred to Cinnaminson High School, but, due to her medical condition, she was on home-bound instruction and never actually attended the school. In fact, we used to tease her that when she graduated from high school, instead of getting a picture of the school she had attended, she would receive a picture of our dining room, where she was tutored most of her high school years.

Not being in school and not having the security of being connected to her friends from school, she found a new group of friends: kids who did not go to school regularly — or at all — and, worse yet, who were involved with drugs. Drugs were common to

Joy. Many drugs had been administered and prescribed to her since she was six. By the end of her original stay in the hospital in 1982, she had had 42 general surgeries. Since she had taken drugs for pain management for months on end, drugs did not frighten her. However, they scared me to death. Drugs were the enemy I had dreaded and hoped never to confront. The pendulum was swinging back and I knew the day would come for Joy to live out her anger.

I didn't have hard evidence of her involvement with drugs, but most of her friends had changed as did her behavior. She was sneaking out at night, staying out all night and sometimes coming home a few days later. I didn't need to know more than this to know that she was involved in a lifestyle that could claim her life whether physically, emotionally, or psychologically. Drugs were a demon to which I was not willing to surrender my daughter.

In retrospect, I did some things I would absolutely advise against. For instance, she had her own telephone in her room, which meant she could make plans to meet her new friends somewhere, or for them to pick her up at the end of our driveway in the middle of the night. She would climb in and out a window so that we did not hear the door being opened. In many ways, Joy was not disabled. The same strong will that helped save her life was now engaged in accomplishing things that could destroy her. In hindsight, I would not give a teenager his/her own phone or cell phone unless I felt totally confident that the people on the other end were not predators looking to lure her with the thrill and temporary excitement of drugs and sex. Predators can be familiar figures — even classmates. It is difficult to compete with what drugs and sex offer. Joy was not a victim, but a willing participant. Nevertheless, I stupidly gave her some of the means to help accomplish this new life: money, a phone and a car. She was well equipped to be someone a predator could eagerly welcome into his or her club.

An added note to parents: I would advise you to be alert. Once you realize that something is wrong in your child's behavior, take immediate steps to understand it, and then stop it! Always know who your child's friends are. Get their phone numbers even if you have to invade your child's so-called privacy. Go into his/her room and search for the information you may desperately need one day. "Snooping" was a godsend for us in the following scenario.

After not being able to locate Joy for a few days, I sought out one of her high school friends who in confidence had given me a phone number. It was the number of an older guy who would host drug parties for younger kids. I was given only a phone number and told that no address was available, because this guy and his mother had recently moved to a neighboring town. After looking up the name of a pizza place in the same town as the phone number given to me, I placed a call to the home. I told the person answering the phone that I was from the local pizza place and that as a promotion to welcome new people into the town, we were offering two free pizzas delivered directly to the newcomers. BUT, first he had to verify his address, which he happily did. Now that I knew where the house was located, I called the local police and had them meet me at the house. Within 20 minutes the police, my over six-foot-tall and very muscular nephew, Tim, his weight-lifter friend, and I arrived at the house. Once again, we took Joy home. Months later Joy asked me how I ever found her at that house. I asked her, "How was the pizza?" She stared at me in disbelief, "That was you?" she asked in amazement as I nodded and smiled.

I was fortunate enough to learn through experience to start calling friends at the first sign that my child could be in danger. Even though teens are loyal to their friends, there usually will be one or more who know the dangers of a child's involvement and will help you. A friend can be the only lifeline a parent has to save a child from drugs. A teen's friends see the changes in their friend and have a sense when it has gone too far and often want to help. Parents need only show these teens how they can. It is hard to imagine that one's own child is lying to this degree, but sometimes teenagers may be too scared or ashamed to admit the whole truth.

I was never going to let go. I would do everything to keep Joy from drugs. I knew the reality was that the drugs might win. I was most amazed that the mothers of some kids involved in drugs would lie for them. One evening after doing my "homework" in my attempt to find Joy, I arrived at a home where kids would gather to socialize and do their drugs. I knocked on the door and the mother of the kids who lived there opened it. By this time, the "kids" Joy was hanging around with were not only high school age, but also in their twenties and quite seasoned in the drug world. I asked the mother to please get my daughter for me. This mother insisted my daughter was not there even though I knew she was. I told the woman she had five minutes to get my daughter out of her house or I was going to set her house on fire. I pointed to the five gallon container of gasoline I had brought with me so she knew I was serious. She went and got Joy.

If I could not keep Joy from these so-called friends, I would let them know that I would be showing up and making trouble for them. If Joy would not let go of these drug-abusing friends herself, I would bring enough trouble to them to convince them to let go of her. Not foolish enough to go looking for Joy alone, I often persuaded my nephew, Tim, with his friends to go along. Usually Tim's physical appearance alone made my adversaries take me seriously.

Joy was not in the least threatened by me. We even had physical altercations. She had reached a point where nothing was going to stop her from doing what she wanted to do and she was as determined as I was. Once my husband and I flew to Notre Dame to see a football game. Our being out of town gave Joy another opportunity to do her own thing. Upon arriving in South Bend, I called home to tell the kids that we had arrived safely. Only a few hours had passed since we had left New Jersey, but Tina informed me that Joy was already missing, and that she knew where she was. I calculated that Joy knew we would be gone three days and that gave her three days to party. I called the airline and booked the next flight home, then called the local police to let them know that a group of truant teens were at a particular house doing drugs and asked them to meet me there. The police knew of this house and arrived there first. The policeman knocked on the door of the house and asked to see Joy. The policeman explained to Joy that I was on my way to this house. In Joy's cockiest tone, she said, "My mother is not here. She's in Indiana." Before Joy had finished her statement, I drove up in the car. Joy was shocked to see me. I took her home once again.

None of this was easy. Many times after an episode with Joy and her druggie friends, I would return home emotionally spent and physically exhausted from the late night. I would then retreat to the unused room on the second floor that was set up as my husband's home office and drop to my knees sobbing, knowing only God understood. My only hope was in the fact that the Lord always knew what Joy was doing and where she would be next, but I was still terrified for her.

In a drawer in my husband's desk, I had placed my Bible and a list of scripture verses that were special to me in these times of utter despair. My fears for Joy and her life were so real and terrifying that often when I came to this room to pray, I could not. So I would take my Bible and the scripture verses out of the drawer and through my tears, I would read them over and over to myself:

"Be strong and courageous. Do not be terrified; do not be discouraged, for the Lord your God will be with you wherever you go."

Joshua 1:9

"When you pass through the waters,
I will be with you;
and when you pass through the rivers
they will not overcome you.
When you walk through the fire,
you will not be burned;
the flames will not set you ablaze
For I am the Lord, your God."

Isaiah 43: 2&3

And then I would read Psalm 121, focusing on verses 1&2
"I lift up my eyes to the hills-
where does my help come from?
My help comes from the Lord."

I was no longer in control of Joy's life as I was when she was a child. Joy was old enough now to make her own decisions. I could not stop her from doing drugs and I could not keep her away from the people who did. She was playing with fire and I could only pray that God would keep the dangerous flames of the drugs from setting her ablaze with desire and claiming her body and mind.

In my desperate search for help, I began looking for a church to attend; someone suggested Calvary Chapel of Philadelphia in Bensalem, Pennsylvania, which was about 40 minutes from my home. I went alone. That Sunday morning as Pastor Joe Focht spoke from God's word, I was overcome with emotion. I realized that although I was searching for a place to take Joy for help, that God was calling me home, to church. Week after week, I was comforted, encouraged, blessed and challenged by Pastor Joe's message from the Bible which I felt was specific to my needs. It felt good to be back in the house of the Lord. Joy came with me occasionally.

However, nothing about the situation with Joy seemed to change. I continued spending many nights out of the house looking for her and retrieving her, only to start all over again the next night or sometimes a few hours later. Sadly, I often had to rely on Tina for help, but she never complained. She understood the drug culture —not because she was involved in it, but because it was the culture of the day. Drugs were not just a part of poverty. They were a big part of the present day privileged teen's life, and I hated that drugs robbed control and good judgment from their victims. My journey with Joy was far from over. I remained committed to seeing life through with Joy and trying to rescue her from herself. She was a good student and still had a chance to go to college.

Finally, by Joy's senior year, it seemed that things were settling down enough for Joy to apply for college. She was accepted at Trenton State College, now the College of New Jersey, to study nursing. To me, she appeared like any other freshman going to college and I was excited for her new beginning. However, faced with adapting to college life and other personal challenges that I was unaware of at the time, attending college became too difficult for her and she left at the end of her second year.

Chapter Thirty-Seven

A Welcomed Addition

When Joy left college, she went back to her life of using drugs and staying out all night. Although Joy's adventures occupied most of my time and energy, I did not feel that I could allow them to consume the rest of the family. After all, my new stepfamily had not lived through the initial trauma with us and could not possibly understand what we went through to save Joy's life. How could they possibly be expected to understand and be compassionate towards this era in her life? Her irresponsible behavior was embarrassing to us all.

Although my husband was extremely supportive, I tried to isolate him from the events as much as I could by keeping the details of her episodes to a minimum. I felt that she was my responsibility, as were the problems she was creating. However, some incidents were brought right to the forefront. Like the time she and a companion pulled into a gas station to get gas knowing they had no money. After the attendant pumped the gas, the two sped away. We got the call to come pick her up at the police station. Lucky for her, the gas attendant was only interested in being paid for the gas and did not press charges.

Lar, now 29 years old, was the first to voice his resentment towards Joy's behavior. Although he had moved out of the house to finish college and then graduate school, he was somewhat aware of what Joy was doing. He let me know that he and his siblings had been raised to respect their father and his position as a lawyer and a judge and my daughter was behaving in a despicable manner. I could only agree. Having a stepdaughter using illegal drugs and running with a crowd of delinquents was not only abhorrent to Larry but could possibly jeopardize his career. Needless to say, my husband did not deserve to have someone living in his home who had such a disregard for his position. I was busy doing serious search and rescue all night with Joy, and during the day I was a business woman, a member of the township committee and the wife of a Superior Court Judge. But more than all of these things, I was Joy's mother. Nevertheless, I was not willing to look the other way and excuse her behavior. I was willing to rescue her from herself to a certain degree, but if a price had to be paid for her defiance of authority, she would pay it.

And then her carelessness caught up with her. Almost predictably, Joy became pregnant. When Joy told me she was pregnant, I was not surprised, but felt that having a child could be too difficult and demanding for her physically. I was not happy that Joy chose this way to bring a child into the world and to begin having a family of her own. However this child did not know that there was anything wrong with the way he was arriving, so in God's grace, with much prayer and a ton of love and forgiveness, our family set out to support the birth and health of both the child and mother.

I knew Joy's would be a high-risk pregnancy, so we immediately consulted the Department of Maternal Fetal Medicine at the University of Pennsylvania. One concern was that Joy, not realizing she was pregnant, had already been given antibiotics for an infection and morphine for pain; she would continue to need antibiotics throughout her pregnancy. Joy's continuous need for antibiotics was due to frequent infections as a result of her thin grafted skin and her own perspiration. The skin, especially on her long leg, would break down and open sores would break out. These sores could not heal because they were always damp from perspiration which occurred from the heat from her body, the thickness of the wool stump socks, the stump socket and the leg itself. Often times, the perspiration that had accumulated in the bottom of Joy's prosthesis would be of such a large amount that she could actually pour the perspiration out of her prosthesis.

Not wearing her prostheses was not an acceptable option for Joy. When Joy did not wear her prostheses, she would maneuver around the house "walking" on her knees, which was very hard on them. Although great strides had been made in the field of prosthetics, Joy's skin had not improved and her adult height and weight, although she was slender, caused problems for her stumps and skin.

Another pregnancy-related issue was Joy's circulatory problems. It is relatively common for a pregnant woman to accumulate fluid in her legs; however this condition would particularly compromise the fit of Joy's prostheses since they were custom made to the size of her stumps. If the size of her stumps changed, the prostheses would not properly fit; therefore her ambulation would be effected. New prostheses could be made, but the cost for a second set of legs could be prohibitive.

What an education I received attending prenatal visits with Joy! When I was pregnant back in 1970, I did not have the knowledge about my pregnancy that Joy had. It was comforting to be so informed, especially since Joy had so many prior medical complications and the doctors were being so cautious.

On one particular visit, Joy had an ultrasound. On the screen, I could actually see a little heart beating in her womb. The exchange of love between this tiny heart and mine was instantaneous. I fell in love with this tiny person. All that was shameful or hurtful was forgotten. A new life was on its way and I would be celebrating.

Joy's pregnancy was normal. Although she did not gain an unusual amount of weight, carrying those extra 25 pounds became difficult for Joy, but she managed to walk right up to delivery. The baby was due February 3 but decided to be born on January 27, 1997; he weighed 6 pounds 7 ounces and had a full head of curly brown hair. As I held Jacob in my arms for the first time, I remembered the dying little girl who I prayed would live to be somebody's grandmother. Joy was on her way to that dream I had for her back then in 1982.

After a normal labor and delivery and a 48-hour overnight stay in the hospital to make sure that Jacob was fine, Joy and her son went to stay with Tina. Tina had purchased my mother's townhouse seven miles away from our Cinnaminson home in Lumberton. Thank God for Tina! Once again, she sacrificed herself, and now her privacy, to help Joy.

Joy set up her bedroom so that it would accommodate her style of caring for her child through the night. She could not put Jacob in a crib because she could not lift him out of it without her legs on and she did not want to have to put them on in the middle of the night. So she pushed her double bed up against the wall so that he would not fall out of it and put Jacob in bed with her. On her night stand next to her bed, she had a good supply of disposable diapers, baby wipes, two-ounce disposable bottles filled with formula and a diaper bag filled with changes of clothing and receiving blankets ready to care for his every need. Beside her bed was a small trash can to take care of all the disposable items. When Jacob awakened, she never had to get out of bed to care for him. Should she have needed help, Tina was right in the next room. This sleeping arrangement continued for a long time and developed an amazing and lasting bond between mother and child, as well as a strong sense of security for her child.

Although the father of the child was in the picture at the time, he had absolutely no means to support Joy and a baby, or himself for that matter. Realizing this, Joy began to make a plan for herself and her child. To my great relief, she had completely stopped using illegal drugs when she discovered that she was pregnant. She was serious about this new responsibility. In recent years, I had not recognized her as the daughter to whom I had taught right from wrong. I had even wondered if she had ever heard anything I said concerning God and His plan for how we should live. Now, she had someone else to think about, her child. She returned to her values and embraced this baby and the responsibility of raising him.

After the birth of Jacob, Joy and I set out to find a new prosthetist for her. After all, she would soon be chasing after a toddler and she needed the best possible set of prostheses to help her. I called the 52 Association, hoping that they could recommend someone, and was delighted to hear that there was someone in Hicksville, New York, who was doing wonders with amputees who were a difficult fit like Joy. The name of the company was A Step Ahead and Erik Schaffer was the owner and person to talk to about Joy. Joy made an appointment and, accompanied by Tina, Jacob and me, went to New York.

We were not disappointed. New technology had improved both the fit and design of prostheses. Joy no longer needed the strap to hold her leg on, but the leg was instead held firmly in place with a pin between the socket and the prostheses. The liners were now made of a new material that actually promoted healing of the skin, Joy's biggest problem. And the prosthetic feet were now being made from a rubber that stored energy similar to a super–ball that bounces extremely high with seemingly great energy when it is thrown to the floor. This amazing amount of "stored" energy in the feet would allow Joy and other amputees an easier and quicker movement. We were thrilled to have found Erik. However, the cost of her new legs was amazing as well, $50,000. But, then what would any of us be willing to pay to walk? Whatever the cost, we knew it would give Joy the active life she yearned for.

Joy received her new legs just in time to attend a family wedding. The church was on a small hill and instead of using the sidewalk after the wedding to return to our car, we decided to go down the grassy hill which was a shorter distance to our vehicle. Hills of this nature were not usually a problem for Joy to navigate, but we underestimated her new energy feet. Joy started down the hill and picked up a head of steam running and cried out to Tina and me, "Help! Jump in front of me so that I can stop before I get to the road!" Luckily Tina's outfit for the wedding allowed her to move much more quickly than I. Tina, running ahead of Joy and spreading her arms out to provide something for Joy to latch onto, successfully broke Joy's stampede and got her stopped. Mission accomplished. On to the reception.

By January of 1997, things could not have been more hectic for me. Jacob was born, my husband had knee replacement surgery and I was sworn in as Mayor of Cinnaminson. And of course, I was still running the salon. The nights I did not have a township meeting, I would come home from work, make dinner, take care of Larry, and then drive to Tina's to help take care of my new grandson. Jacob was a delightful baby who already had a charming way about him. It was easy to bond with him; he would peer so deeply into my eyes that I thought we could see each other's souls. He was precious to me.

A few months passed, and Joy asked for a job at the salon as a receptionist. She would bring Jacob with her. I agreed. But, one particular day at work, Joy was obviously weak and feverish with the flu. I had no choice. I had to take her and two month old Jacob home with me. Although my husband expressed his objection to this new arrangement, he did understand my dilemma. With both Joy and the baby needing care, Larry recovering from surgery, and my other obligations, I could not be stretched any thinner than I already was. I had to get everybody who needed my help under one roof.

It was nice having Mom next door, and she enjoyed helping Joy take care of Jacob. My mother was always sympathetic towards Joy's struggles and her endless suffering. And now, Mom's respect for Joy grew out of Joy's deep desire to raise her child.

Mom and Pop ate most of their evening meals with us and Jacob was our main entertainment at the dinner table. One night after Larry said grace, he raised his hand to his forehead in a salute as he started to sing, "God Bless America". As Larry watched Jacob for his reaction, the rest of us at the table took Larry's lead, saluted and sang along. Jacob, only nine months old, watched his Poppy and imitated his salute by raising his tiny hand to his forehead and joining in with the rest of us. Next Jacob began making sounds in an attempt to sing along. We all laughed hysterically at Jacob. Every night from that point on, we would say grace before our meal, and then like little soldiers, salute and sing "God Bless America". We were all hysterical watching this tiny little boy salute and pretend to sing. This simple humor and lightheartedness was so good for all of us, especially my mother, because Jacob gave

Mom a reason to laugh.

Everyone loved Jacob. He was the common denominator that brought us all together. He instantly had five young-adult aunts and uncles, grandparents and great-grandparents advocating for him. I guess because Joy was a single mom, we all filled in for the parent who was missing in his life. Joy was such a loving mother and was so respectful of our many suggestions about how to raise her child. One day as she was seeking my advice on parenting, I had the opportunity to tell her what a fabulous job she was doing raising Jacob. In fact, I confessed, she was a much better mother day-to-day than I ever was. I considered myself privileged to observe the love affair that was going on between my daughter and her child.

Being a good mother meant a great deal to Joy, and in that role, she felt responsible to help her child grow in the knowledge of God. Joy began looking into joining Larry's church since she and Jacob had already been attending Mass with Larry. Larry had also been talking to Joy about getting Jacob baptized. Therefore, Joy approached Rob, a lector at his neighboring parish, to sponsor her in the RCIA (Rite of Christian Initiation for Adults) program at St. Charles Borromeo Roman Catholic Church in Cinnaminson so that Joy could join the Church. In 1999 at the Easter Vigil Liturgy at St. Charles Borromeo, Joy received the Sacraments of Confirmation, Holy Communion and, along with Jacob, Baptism.

Joy with Jacob at two years old

Chapter Thirty-Eight

Heaven Bound

My mother's diabetes progressed and the effects on her body and mind became serious. Since Mom was a nurse, she clearly understood what was happening to her. Due to the progression of her diabetes, Mom knew that one day she would lose her leg, which happened all too soon in 1996. The day of the amputation was a tragic day for her, but she would not admit to her own grief. Her response to the loss of her limb was, "Do you know who my granddaughter is? Well, if she can deal with it, so can I!" Who could argue with that? In our family we were experts at amputations, sores, swelling, stumps, stump socks, prostheses — anything an amputee needed to know. In fact, we had at least seven spare legs lying around our house.

After Mom's leg was amputated (below the knee), Joy and her grandmother became soul mates. Joy became very involved in her grandmother's care through her recovery and gave her on-going pointers on how to adjust to wearing a prothesis and the daily routine of putting just enough stump socks on to make the leg feel comfortable. Although Mom did get a prothesis, she was never successful walking.

Joy's bond with her grandmother was out of respect for what each of them had lost — a limb. They both understood that every morning when they got ready to get out of bed, their feet would never touch the floor. They also both experienced the pain of open sores on their stumps and the pain that rain and humidity brought to their bones. Together they shared a campaign to refuse to let the world and narrow thinking define them. It was wonderful that they had each other to lean on.

Much too soon, Mom was diagnosed with congestive heart failure, another complication of her diabetes. She and Pop had been spending the winters in Florida, but now the disease had progressed enough that shortly after Mom and Pop returned to New Jersey in April 1999, her shortness of breath made frequent emergency trips to the hospital necessary. It is frightening watching someone gasping for air. Each time we called, the ambulance and its volunteers responded immediately, took all the appropriate steps, including giving Mom oxygen, and then drove her to the hospital. And each time I was relieved, although surprised, she made it.

Due to Mom's medical history, especially her increasing dementia as a result of her diabetes, surgery was not an option and in Mom's heart, she knew the time had come to let the Lord decide when He would call her home. This is not a decision for the cowardly, but for those who recognize that when the body can no longer survive, the soul still has a destination.

Hospice was called in and along with the hospice nurses, Pop, Joy and I began taking care of Mom. There was tremendous sadness for us in this process, yet a superb honor in serving this wonderful woman in her final days on earth. My dear mother was fading quickly and after only two weeks on hospice, Mom was completely bedridden. Tina returned from Florida where she had relocated, to help care for the grandmother she adored.

After an exhausting two weeks, we asked my brother Ed and his wife, Carol, and my sister Kay to help care for Mom, which they gladly did, by taking a shift in the round-the-clock care. In fact, Carol devised a plan of care that was so thoughtful, my mother herself, who had been trained in how to prevent bedsores in bedridden patients, would have sung Carol's praises. Carol was meticulous and sensitive in planning my mother's care and we all lovingly implemented her suggestions.

As a family, we came together to serve this wonderful woman and to show our love and share our faith. One day as Mom's children and grandchildren were gathered around her hospital bed in the living room of the guest house, my brother led us in prayer thanking God for the loving mother that He chose for us and expressing how grateful we all were for the promise of seeing her again when we ourselves would join her in heaven. Our family tearfully joined in singing Mom's favorite hymn, "How Great Thou Art".

We continued caring for Mom with the help of additional nurses, but this one particular day it was up to us to bathe Mom and she was now comatose. Four granddaughters, all in their twenties —Joy, Tina, Courtney Kanner and Cassie Fowler — quietly and reverently took their places around my mother's bed with Kay and Carol preparing to bathe, turn and dress my mother. I gazed in wonder at this scene. This quiet, shy, unpretentious woman was being attended to by these young women of our family in such a regal fashion. I was captivated by the gentle and purposeful ceremonious manner they touched her body, a ritual befitting a queen. In their gestures of kindness and reverence towards my mother, it was obvious that they believed her worthy of their love and respect.

My beloved mother passed on into glory on July 28,1999. What a blessing to have wonderful friends and family for those difficult times in life. It is very sad to say good-bye to someone you dearly love, someone who has been there for you all of your life, who nurtured and cared for you and loved you unconditionally. As sad as her passing was to me personally, I knew that what was most dear to my mother—her abiding faith in the Lord and her steadfast devotion to her family —would live on in us, her children.

Joy eulogized her grandmother at her funeral and in so doing praised her for her strength and her persistence to overcome her own hardships in her younger years. Joy said she was grateful for having the privilege of knowing her so well and for the examples she set for all of us, demonstrating the importance of remaining faithful to God and family.

Joy then told an amusing yet endearing story of the kind of relationship of trust and honesty that Joy and her grandmother shared:

"I wanted to take a turn staying with Grandmom through the night when she was so ill. So I told my mother that she should go lie down on the sofa in the back room and I would call her if Grandmom needed anything. My mother was beyond exhaustion with being up so many nights with Grandmom, so I wanted to give her some relief, but I really wanted to be alone with my Grandmom whom I loved so very much. I sent Jacob to the main house with Poppy. Then I sat on the edge of Grandmom's hospital bed, took my legs off, let them drop to the floor and put my arms around my Grandmother, hoping to comfort her and in all honesty, to comfort myself, too. She was everything to me and when she lost her leg, we became even closer.

"Grandmom was on morphine for her discomfort, but in the past had become disoriented from taking the drug, so I held her close to me, hoping that she knew that I was there with her. At some point in the middle of the night, Grandmom became very restless. Although I tried to calm her, her anxiety was peaking and she was now trying to get out of the bed. In a low voice hoping to quiet her down, I tried to explain to her that she was not able to get out of bed or stand on her own for that matter, but she persisted in trying to get out of the bed.

"Frustrated with the situation, I raised my voice and in a loud tone I yelled, `Grandmom, you have to stay in bed! How far do you think you're going to get? We only have one leg between the two of us!'

"Instantly Grandmom settled down and opted to stay in bed. She seemed to understand our dilemma.

"Grandmom and I shared a few laughs over our ongoing problems with our stumps and our prostheses…and many tears. I can truly say, she understood how I felt. So Grandmom, today in heaven I know you now have your new legs and when I get there, I will be looking forward to running all over heaven with you on my new legs."

§§§

Jacob was only two years old at my mother's funeral, but he was a child who paid attention to what was said. A few months had passed since that very sad occasion, and Larry, Jacob and I were in the car, stopped at a red light. From our car we could see runners from Moorestown's annual 5 Mile Rotary Run that was being held on Main Street. Hundreds of runners passed in front of our car. I turned to look at Jacob in his car seat in the backseat. I was surprised by the look on his face: he was absolutely spellbound by the spectacle of all of these people running by. I could not imagine why his eyes were so glued on these runners.

Finally, but for one brief second, I got his attention and asked him why he was staring at the runners. As serious as could be and with unmistakable exuberance, he pointed in the direction of the people running in the race and exclaimed, "Look, Grammy! That must be heaven. Everyone is running around just like my Mommy said GiGi (Jacob's name for my mother) is doing in heaven."

Joy and Grandmom

Chapter Thirty-Nine

The Announcement

Almost every day before work, Larry and I would drive about three miles to the parking lot of the Riverton Yacht Club on the Delaware River to have our morning coffee. As soon as Jacob could sit up, he joined us. "Poppy" began educating Jacob about the pleasures of fishing, swimming, duck hunting, and sailing that could be enjoyed at the river. Poppy told Jacob how much the river meant to him as a young boy and how he had embraced every aspect of the river's charm and every creature it could entice. Poppy told these stories with such passion that even this young child could recognize how special these memories were for Poppy. Discovering that Jacob shared his interest in the river, Poppy was delighted to unfold the mysteries of the river to him.

Poppy was already influencing this less than one-year-old to become an outdoorsman as Larry had been in his youth. Larry often regretted giving up the things that he enjoyed as a young boy to engross himself in his professional life. Jacob became his grandfather's best student as he listened so intently to everything Poppy said and Poppy was glad to be his mentor. I realized through listening to Larry's dialog that the set of instructions Larry was giving his grandson about what to enjoy and how to set priorities were not the instructions he had given his children. For Jacob, Larry emphasized the joy of life, not just academic achievement. I too wanted Jacob to enjoy his life and the things that brought peace and harmony to the soul.

Joy was now attending a community college that accepted her credits from her former college and, with a few additional classes, she earned an associate's degree in Sociology. She had hopes of going back someday to finish her Bachelor of Science degree, but for now she was a full-time mom.

When Jacob turned two, Joy began working at a pre-school where she could also take Jacob. The owner of the pre-school, Tina Schulz, and Joy became very close friends. This relationship and this job gave Joy something exciting and fulfilling to look forward to each day as she pursued her love of nurturing children. Joy was absolutely wonderful with children and was never bored around them. In fact, being with children so agreed with her that at the end of a day of work, she would actually glow. I admired her desire to raise her own children. I found it interesting that my generation of women wanted careers and her generation wanted to stay home with their children. Through Jacob, I could see in Joy the return of the person I had known before — a kind, giving, loving, and patient human being.

Someone else noticed it too. He noticed Joy as she redefined herself as a woman and a mother, and he already noticed and enjoyed the antics and love Jacob brought to our family.

That year, some happy events were taking place in our lives, which called for the family to get together on a regular basis. One such happy occasion was the upcoming wedding of Larry's daughter Gloria to Keith Ruscitti in November 1998. Lar, Larry's oldest son, came back home to Cinnaminson for the events leading up to the wedding. Lar was in the wedding as was his brother Rob who, after obtaining his masters degree in mathematics from Villanova University, was teaching mathematics in a high school in North Jersey. Two-year-old Jacob was to be the ring bearer. We were all very excited about this day and so happy for Gloria and Keith as a couple. Keith's light heartedness and ability to see any situation with a calming manner made him a wonderful addition to our family.

No one but me seems to recall this event, but at one point during the wedding reception, Lar asked another guest who the beautiful blonde was who was dancing and having the time of her life. That guest turned to Lar in utter amazement and responded, "That's Joy!" It seemed to Lar that he was seeing her for the first time in his life.

In January, Joy and Lar went out for a drink to celebrate his birthday. Lar had just turned 35 and Joy was 25. Lar was a very private person and had been living at the shore for the past few years while he was finishing his MBA at Rowan University in Glassboro, New Jersey. He was still a big part of our family, but as a young man trying to determine his future, he kept pretty much to himself. However, he enjoyed being with Jacob and would make a point of spending time with him when he did come home.

In early February, Lar was home to pick up some mail and have dinner with the family. During dinner Lar announced he would be applying for a teaching position at Rancocas Valley Regional High School (RVRHS) in Mt. Holly in the business education department. Since Lar already had an accounting degree from Rutgers University and now his MBA, we agreed this was a good career choice for him. Lar knew of the high school's great reputation from his sister Glor who was teaching special education at RVRHS while working on her master's degree at Georgian Court University. After the kitchen was cleaned up, and Lar had left, my husband and I decided to relax at the kitchen table, each reading a portion of the morning paper that we had not had time to read earlier in the day.

Suddenly, Lar appeared in the kitchen. It was strange for me not to hear him re-enter the house, but now I noticed that he seemed a little edgy and distracted as he paused at the end of the kitchen cabinets and leaned against them staring at the refrigerator. He began nervously pacing back and forth. He clearly had something on his mind. First he got something out of the cabinet, then the refrigerator and then back to the cabinet; next he paused and leaned against the counter again, obviously in deep thought. Then he drew a deep breath and studied his father and me seated at the table only a few feet from where he was propped against the counter.

Out of the corner of my eye, I continued watching Lar and sensed that he was troubled and possibly had something he needed to say. I did not want to press Lar to speak, and my husband was engrossed in the newspaper, completely oblivious to Lar's unusual behavior. Trying to relieve his suffering and help this situation move forward, I asked Lar if something was on his mind, and he cautiously responded, "Yes." I was prepared to leave the table and let father and son have their discussion when Lar sat down at the table across from me. His father, my husband, was seated at the head of the table to my left still reading the paper— as usual. And, as usual, I thought Larry should put the newspaper down and listen to what his son had to say, but Lar's father seemed spellbound by something in the paper. Anyway, Larry always told me he could read and listen at the same time.

Lar looked straight at me, swallowed hard, and confessed, "Joy and I have been seeing each other and ..."

Before he could finish his sentence, I exploded. "What?!" I exclaimed in total shock. I stared in amazement at my husband who was STILL reading the paper. Didn't Larry hear what Lar just said? Lar hadn't even finished his sentence, but I knew I had to jump in and put an end to this! Inside my head I was shouting: *"Oh no, you two! I will not allow a little fling between the two of you to destroy our family! Get over it and move on! Both of you."*

My mind was racing, as I struggled to comprehend this new situation. Trying to be rational, I reminded myself that Joy and Lar were not related. And there isn't really anything wrong with their dating, but still this revelation seemed so sudden and so preposterous. As I began to think through all the arguments against their having a relationship, I realized there was more Lar wanted to say. I knew I had better start listening carefully to what Lar was telling us since I WAS the only parent listening.

Now Lar paused for a moment. Watching my face closely and choosing his words carefully, he blurted out the rest of his announcement "… and we are in love and want to get married."

My jaw dropped and I stared in disbelief. Looking relieved to get this off his chest, Lar patiently waited for me to absorb this latest development.

My mind still reeling, I quickly registered that I had heard the words "in love" which to me meant it was much too late to change things.

And, at long last, the father peeped over the edge of the newspaper to say absently, "Love, that's a good thing."

My husband's reaction confirmed that I was on my own here. *Where is Joy?* I found myself wondering.

Next, I asked Lar what their plans were. Because they had known each other so long, a lengthy engagement seemed not necessary or even advisable. He, of course, agreed to discuss it with Joy, but moving forward soon was what they had talked about.

It suddenly occurred to me that Lar was doing the old-fashioned thing by asking for Joy's hand in marriage. How honorable. Still I continued asking myself: *Where is Joy?* I was determined to see that she was not just leading on this wonderful guy. I got up and charged into the parlor to quiz my daughter.

Joy and Jacob were on the floor, happily engrossed in watching TV and playing together with his toys. Joy saw me standing in the doorway to the parlor with a stern look on my face and quietly asked, "What's wrong?" I told Jacob to go see Poppy so that he would not hear our "private" conversation and then I enlightened Joy of Lar's revelation.

Joy scrambled to a chair helplessly sputtering some inane explanations when she suddenly realized that no excuse was necessary for this situation. Although she did not agree with Lar's timing, his profession of their love for each other and their plans for marriage were indeed correct. She could chide Lar later for his timing, but right now, the four of us had some talking to do.

We retrieved Jacob from his Poppy in the kitchen and put on his favorite video while the four of us, Larry, Lar, Joy and I continued our conference in the kitchen. Now that the shock had subsided, Larry and I needed to discuss what we could do to help them plan the wedding and set the date.

That evening as I pondered this unusual union, I realized that, once again, the Lord had answered my prayers. I would often talk to the Lord about the man he would send for Joy to marry. She was certainly attractive enough: charming, focused, strong-willed, loving and a great mother, to name a few things. But could there ever be a man in her life who understood what her life was like when she took her legs off and crawled around the house? Could he really deal with her disfigurement and love her the way I wanted him to love and cherish her? Could he ever understand her struggles, her many, many surgeries and the young life she had missed because of them? Could any man know the sacrifices she had had to make? How could I ever put into words what happened to her and what she needed to do every day to make her life go on? The right man for Joy needed to have been there to completely understand her suffering. He needed to have been there to see that no matter how she gets around, on her legs or on her knees, that she is independent, bold and self-confident. He needed to have been a part of her life when she was going through these things to really understand...

And Larry's wonderful son, Lar, had been there all along; he DID understand her struggles and her life.

Could the Lord have brought Larry and me together as a means to unite Joy and Lar? God does work in strange and wondrous ways.

The wedding was set for May 19, 2001 and it would be a glorious occasion!

Joy and Lar

Chapter Forty

The Wedding

The day of the wedding began early at Creative Image Salon and Day Spa, where my staff spent hours thinking about and designing the perfect hairstyles and elegant looks we were to wear on this marvelous day. Even our make-up was done to perfection to add just the right finishing touches and to ensure we would remain photogenic all day long. Our nails had been manicured or "filled in" to make them the "perfect ten" the day before, and everyone in the Bridal Party enjoyed a spa pedicure for those open-toed shoes they were wearing. So from head to toe we were pampered and readied for this special day, thanks to the expert staff of Creative Image Salon and Day Spa.

For over 30 years, my salons had been putting the finishing touches on brides and their bridal parties. Today this particular bride, Joy, was fussed over like no other bride had ever been. This salon's staff had watched Joy and Tina grow up over the years. They became even better acquainted with Tina when she joined our salon as office manager. Ronnie Cherbonnie, our receptionist, had always consummately answered the staff's and the clients' questions of "How is Joy doing? How's Tina? How does Karen cope with all of this?" Ronnie always responded in her usual warm and sensitive manner. Debbie Kramer was also incredibly special to our family. Although Debbie herself was a very busy and committed mother and grandmother, she sincerely understood my constant dilemmas concerning Joy and would rush to assist me in every possible way. Her artistic talent in all aspects of the beauty business was outstanding. I always felt confident recommending Debbie to any clients, knowing that they would receive a superb service from her. Christine Kenkelen, our seasoned shampoo assistant who ran the salon behind the scenes was certainly an important part of this day.

As the chatter of the day took hold, the bridal party members — Maid of Honor Tina, Bridesmaids Mindy Gensler, Gloria Eleuteri Ruscuitti, Liz Besnoff, and Karen Gappa — were excitedly exchanging stories about Joy and her many escapades. Liz in particular reminisced about what close friends she and Joy had become when Jacob was born and Liz would often stop by to visit with them. These were Joy's most cherished supporters. They were a special part of this day to give witness to this unimaginable turn of events in Joy's life. Finally, the "Joy Story" had a happy ending. They were all thrilled to be standing for her as they had done so many times before and for so many reasons. I was glad for this day for Joy's sake, but I was also hoping this day would bring about a new beginning for Tina. I was her mother too. Maybe she could get on with her own life now — a life apart from her worrying constantly about Joy.

Joy's two-year-old flower girl, Anne Larkin, a cousin of Lar's, thought playing beauty shop and getting all dressed up for this occasion was not much fun. After some deliberation with Anne as to how she should have her hair done, Anne chose to wear her hair "au natural". This was one bridal party of independent women that could appreciate another independent thinking woman, even if she was only two.

The groom, Lar, and his brother Rob, had stayed the night before the wedding at a local hotel in order to provide a place for Lar and his groomsmen to don their tuxedos. This left the house for the girls. Girly things were strewn throughout the house. The bridal gown and its accessories seemed to take up my entire dressing room. Bridesmaids' dresses hung from every doorway and the absolutely perfect undergarments, shoes, pantyhose and bulging cases of hair products and make-up filled every chair. Our home was overflowing with beautiful women and all the paraphernalia essential to satisfy their dreams of this joyful and love-filled occasion.

None of these intrusions disturbed Larry. As usual, Larry was a charming host, but knew to stay out of the way of women scurrying about to primp for a big event. The morning slipped by quickly and the wedding was to begin at 11 AM at Saint Charles Borromeo Church where Joy and Lar were both parishioners. The photographer would soon arrive for those special pre-wedding photos of the bride and her attendees. My sister, Kay, was on hand to give us some help, while her daughter Beth, one of the junior bridesmaids, was helping distribute the bouquets of flowers that the girls would carry. Another junior bridesmaid, Taylor Walsh, Joy's cousin from the Spering family, would soon join Beth.

Larry and I finally found time to get ourselves dressed while Jacob had his own " valet," Tara Gallagher, a very attractive twenty-year-old woman who occasionally took care of him. Today Tara's role was to assure that Jacob was properly attired for his place of honor as presenter of the bride.

My excitement peaked when I saw Joy walking down the stairs of our home dressed in her gown and veil. Our home has a large center hall with a three-story staircase that appears specifically designed for a bride's entrance. Joy looked spectacular! Tina followed her down the stairs and I remember thinking how absolutely lovely she looked in her periwinkle two-piece long dress. Close behind them was the rest of the similarly-dressed bridal party. As they reached the last step, I could see the flashes from the photographer's camera that let me know that shortly after these photos were taken, we would all head for the church.

The limousines arrived. I kissed my daughter, wishing her God's blessing on her wedding day as she got into her limousine and headed to the church, which was just around the corner. Jacob and Tina accompanied Joy in the limo. As I watched them pull out of our driveway I thought about the many blessings God had bestowed upon our family and that His presence in our lives was so very obvious to me. I almost felt that an invitation should have been sent to Him, but then, I knew He would be there. After all, this marriage was His idea to start with.

Larry and I then left for the church. Once there, we checked to make sure all was going as planned. Everything was moving along nicely and I felt relieved to have reached this point. The bridal party was assembled at the back of the church. Little Anne looked adorable in her full-skirted off-white floor length "princess" gown. She looked so beautiful it was hardly noticeable that the flowers meant for her baby fine hair were slipping and would soon land on the floor. She did not seem to mind. Tommy Ruscitti, our grandson, arrived handsomely dressed in his very tiny black tuxedo with silver cummerbund and tie. He had just turned two in April. As ring bearer, he had the traditional pillow for the rings clutched very tightly in his small hands, just as rehearsed. He would be the first one down the aisle, or so we prayed. This very long walk with people staring from both sides of the aisle appeared a bit frightening to a little boy, but we knew he would do a great job.

Larry and I, summoned by the music, Pachelbel's Canon in D, walked arm in arm to the front of the church to light a candle together on the altar and then took our place in a front pew. Reverend Thomas Triggs, "Father Tom," soon appeared from the sacristy, the room off the altar in which the sacred vessels and vestments are kept. Lar and his groomsmen came into view ready to take their positions along the front of the altar. Lar's best man, Frank Legg, was a life-long friend from the shore where the Eleuteri family spent many summers at their second home in Bayville, New Jersey. Rob Eleuteri, brother of the groom, along with two of Lar's friends from high school, Michael DiMarco and Daniel Kane, and Joy's cousin, Timothy Fowler, stood patiently awaiting the bride's entrance. The junior groomsmen, eleven-year-old Pierce Bowker, and seven-year-old Nicholas Fowler, Joy's cousins, good looking in their formal attire, gave the impression of very mature young men as they stood erect yet shoulders below "the big guys" next to them.

Now, the time had come. The chords of the familiar Wedding March announced that the bride and her presenter were in place and ready to begin the procession down the aisle. Everyone stood and faced Joy and Jacob. As I quickly glanced at our many friends who had come to celebrate with us, my eye caught a tear that was flowing down my cousin Maureen's face. I suddenly realized that she was not alone in her sentiment on this day, for many eyes, including my own, were glistening with over-flowing emotion and many cheeks were being discreetly wiped. A few of our family members and closest friends were, in fact, quietly sobbing. As solemn a scene as this may have seemed at a wedding, I understood their feelings. This was a very special day for those guests who were familiar with Joy and her years of pain and suffering.

Joy's childhood had been snatched away by a common virus gone awry. Despite the devastation of her young body from this virus, she overcame the threat of death only to live what seemed to be a life filled with endless hospitalizations and surgeries, amputations, and permanent disfigurement, even the shadow of a lifetime in a wheelchair. Any tears shed were of gratitude for the miracles our guests knew they were witnessing on this day.

The miracle of Joy walking again as God had promised her...
...and here she was walking down the aisle on her wedding day.

And then, the miracle of discovering that special person God had chosen as her mate for life. Now, everyone present knew the answer to the question posed by a very ill, six-year-old girl some 20 years earlier after she lost both of her legs to a rare case of chicken pox, "But who will marry me?"

...and there he was, the groom, standing at the front of the church eagerly awaiting the arrival of his bride.

§§§

As I turned once again to face the bride and her son, I had peace in my heart, knowing that Joy was already somebody's mother and someday she would be somebody's grandmother. Through her children and her children's children, she would live on. Why would I choose anything other than that for her? With God in our lives, we all found the strength to endure the pain and suffering of this life. Life is difficult, not impossible.

Thank God!

Joy and Lar at their wedding — 2001

In Loving Memory

Joy Spering
June 1975 - August 2004

After more than two years of writing and editing, I
sent the manuscript for this book to the publisher on August 29, 2004.
It had taken longer than I expected and I had actually submitted it
once before and pulled it back before it could be printed. But I was
finally satisfied with the manuscript and delighted that I was telling
Joy's story — a story of pain and sorrow, but one also of overcoming
adversity with God's help, and eventual triumph.

During the years since her wedding, Joy lived her dream. She and
her husband welcomed two more children into their lives; Elizabeth

Mary was born November 7, 2001, and Peter Lawrence was born on January 6, 2003 (Jacob was born on January 27, 1997.) But the hopes she had for herself and her children were often interrupted by her on-going battles with infections — battles that included an additional eight more inches being amputated from her left leg in an attempt to provide a better delivery of antibiotics to the infected area and thus finally a cure for her chronic infections. Twelve hours after the surgery, which took place on her 28th birthday in 2003, she spiked a fever of 108 degrees (this is not a misprint) and her heart raced at 200 beats a minute. Once again Joy was not expected to live through the night, but being Joy, she triumphed once again, surviving yet another close call with death.

However on August 30, 2004. the morning after the manuscript had been sent to the publisher, Joy collapsed on her bathroom floor and was rushed by ambulance to the hospital. Her husband, Lar, and I waited in the ER waiting room to hear from her doctors, both of us fully expecting them to tell us that Joy would be OK. Although she had been extremely weak and ill, I was confident that she would return home and we would have yet another heroic story to tell about the way Joy always beat the odds. Less than an hour later, however, a nurse quietly asked Lar and me to step into a small room off to the side of the waiting area. After the ER doctor joined us, he told us that Joy had arrived at the hospital with a very weak pulse and that although they had done everything possible, she had not survived. Stunned by what the doctor had just said, I wanted to shout, " No, you don't understand. This is Joy Spering. Joy doesn't die!" But sadly, after 23 years of beating the odds, Joy's time on earth was over.

Over the previous 24 months, I had realized on some level that Joy might actually be losing the battle against the infection in her body. After numerous hospitalizations, doctors' visits and in-home antibiotic therapy (which made her extremely fatigued, nauseous and bed-bound), Joy was being robbed of the quality of life and precious time with her children and husband. Even with massive doses of antibiotics, she did not get better. The periods of her feeling good in between hospitalizations and antibiotic therapy were shortening and there even had been talk of further amputation; she and her doctors were also fearful of her encountering some bacteria that although minor to most people, would be life-threatening to her. I even asked her one day during the summer if she were dying, because it seemed to me that a certain sadness had engulfed her. Joy's response to me was: "Well you know, Mom, I probably won't live to 80."

A few times she said, "Mom, please get the book done, I don't know how much longer I'm going to last." I really did not understand what she meant. I could not imagine that God had called me to write this book and Joy not be alive to celebrate her life's story and God's victories in her life. I dreamed of the day, after this book was published, when, at some gathering where I was invited to speak, I would, at just the right moment in my speech, move my eyes to where Joy was seated in the audience, and, beaming with pride, introduce Joy. Then, as she was rising to her feet, the audience would enthusiastically applaud her. In this dream of mine, I could see Joy's face smiling as she humbly responded to their applause and in her heart, she would rejoice that she had fought so long and hard to get to this moment in her life.

All the time I was writing, I was also praying that the medical profession would find a cure for her infections or that God Himself would heal her. I really did not understand why God was not answering my prayers. But I continued writing this book no matter what else interfered. I would get up at 5 AM to write and I felt that sometimes God would get me up in the middle of the night to write. This surely was His project and I was His willing servant, however tired I became. I was driven to get this done and I kept writing. And although exhausted, day after day Tina and I continued to care for Joy and her children while her husband worked, expecting that at some point Joy would rebound as she always had.

I sensed that I was writing against some unknown time clock. I even said to my husband on more than one occasion, "I don't know what this is all about, but something big is going to happen when I get this book done, I just feel it."

Joy only read the first few chapters in a very early version of the manuscript. Her comment was," Gee, Mom, this is really a great story. But tell me, does the little girl live?" We both chuckled. She never asked me again what I was writing or what I was saying about her in the book. Tina, Joy and I knew that the book was not only Joy's story but the story of a living God who loves us and answers our prayers. In fact this was God's story told through the suffering and victories of one little girl named Joy Spering.

After her passing, I was given a suggested reading from the Bible for her funeral. The verses were from the Book of Job in which Job, who had suffered greatly in his life, pleads with his friend, saying:

> " *Oh, that my words were recorded,*
> *that they were written on a scroll,*
> *that they were inscribed with an iron tool on lead,*
> *or engraved in rock forever!*"

Job 19:23-24

Struck by the realization that I had done just that for Joy,

I suddenly became aware that I had written her story so that her children, especially, might remember her. Also, it occurred to me that like Job, Joy was born to suffer and that her purpose on this earth was determined at the age of six, when she agreed to live her life as a disabled, disfigured and pain-ridden person so that she could show others how, with God's help, people can overcome anything.

I also now believe that Joy wanted her story written while she was still alive so that her story would be told with a celebratory, triumphant tone, not as a sad, retrospective memoir of a little girl who had fought a battle and ultimately lost. Because in the end, Joy did triumph — she lived her life joyously and realized her most heart-felt dreams.

When I had told my husband something big was going to happen when I completed this book, I had been correct. But I never dreamed that something big would be Joy's death from pneumonia. The very next morning after the revised, final manuscript was sent off, after 23 years of hard-won victories over a killer-disease and its relentless aftermath, her body was finally defeated. Joy's book was pulled before printing so I could write about her passing in addition to her triumphs.

Breaking through my grief, Tina made me realize why God did not answer my prayers for Joy to get better. Tina said it was because Joy was praying too — that her Heavenly Father would take her home to be with Him and finally relieve her from all her pain and suffering.

Tina and I can hear Joy's voice as she may have prayed words like these:

> *My dear Lord and Savior, I have lived my dreams*
> *of marrying and having children.*
> *I have also lived and fulfilled my purpose for You.*

*I have suffered tremendously for many years and yet have
been victorious by overcoming the impossible many, many times
which testifies to Your living within me and loving me and
empowering me to go on and keep fighting.
But now, dear Lord, hear my cries. I am tired.
My body cannot go on much longer.
I am weary with the struggle and my mind is forever troubled,
trying desperately to get well.
You have blessed me by giving me these years of life
that I could see my children born.
But now, Lord, I am ready to come home;
to be free of pain, to walk in Your glory on perfect legs
and to end this life of struggle.
Please open Your arms and welcome me
and give me the peace I have been longing for.
As You have filled my life with purpose,
fill me now with the assurance
that I will soon leave this diseased and pain-ridden body
and enter into Your Presence
where I will be more alive than I have ever been.
And comfort my family in their sorrow and grief
by Your promise, that one day we will see each other again
and will live together throughout eternity.
I thank You for never leaving me and I know that You will
never leave my children either.
Although I will not physically be with them,
an ever greater Presence will be with them and that is You.
I am ready to come home.
Your good and faithful servant, Joy.*

God answered her prayer.

Jacob, now seven years old, told me soon after his mother's

passing into glory, "Just think, Grammy, now my Mommy can wiggle her toes." And Eme, almost three years old at the time, says assuredly, "God took Mommy to his home, in heaven." Peter, not quite two years old, sees the wind gently blowing the leaves in the trees, points his finger upward and whispers, "Mommy."

Our family grieves over Joy's passing, but our faith remains strong and our hope lies in the truth that someday, we will all be together in eternity. And until that day, we will live our lives as God has intended.

About the Author

Karen Eleuteri—wife, mother, grandmother, hair salon and day spa owner, former mayor, financial advisor—adds author to her résumé with the publication of this amazing true story, *Step by Step with Joy.*

Karen didn't intend to be an author, but believed that her daughter's story should be documented. Because she knew the story better than anyone, Karen began to write an enlightening memoir about a trying, yet unifying time for her family. What she has written instead is a spiritually uplifting book that retraces how her family met its challenges with grace, tenacity and reliance on God; a book that she hopes can serve as an inspiration for those facing crises in their own lives.

For further information or to contact members of the family, email them at the following addresses. They'll be happy to hear from readers.

keleuteri@comcast.net

tinaspering@comcast.net

Printed in the United States
94249LV00005B/253-300/A

9 781418 482107